For the Love of Cybernetics

For the Love of Cybernetics: Personal Narratives by Cyberneticians is a collection of personal accounts that offer unique insights into cybernetics via the personal journeys of nine individuals.

For the authors in this collection, cybernetics is not their "area of interest" – it is how they think about what they do, and it is their practice. Ray Ison, Bruce Clarke, Frank Galuszka, Paul Pangaro, Klaus Krippendorff, Peter D. Tuddenham, Lucas Pawlik, Bernard Scott, and Jocelyn Chapman differ in their lineage, emphasis, and engagement with cybernetics. What they have in common is that they share the belief that cybernetics is not a tool to apply here and there, but a unifying way of seeing the world that transforms how we behave, thus increasing possibilities for positive systemic change.

This book was originally published as a special issue of the journal, *World Futures*.

Jocelyn Chapman, PhD, is a transdisciplinarian with a special interest in cybernetics and systems thinking. She is the Director of the Transformative Inquiry Department at the California Institute of Integral Studies (CIIS) in San Francisco, USA. She also teaches in the online Transformative Leadership MA and Transformative Studies PhD programs at CIIS.

For the Love of Cybernetics

Personal Narratives by Cyberneticians

Edited by
Jocelyn Chapman

Routledge
Taylor & Francis Group

LONDON AND NEW YORK

First published 2020
by Routledge
2 Park Square, Milton Park, Abingdon, Oxon, OX14 4RN

and by Routledge
52 Vanderbilt Avenue, New York, NY 10017

Routledge is an imprint of the Taylor & Francis Group, an informa business

British Library Cataloguing-in-Publication Data
A catalogue record for this book is available from the British Library

ISBN13: 978-0-367-86101-8

Typeset in Times New Roman
by codeMantra

Publisher's Note
The publisher accepts responsibility for any inconsistencies that may have arisen during the conversion of this book from journal articles to book chapters, namely the inclusion of journal terminology.

Disclaimer
Every effort has been made to contact copyright holders for their permission to reprint material in this book. The publishers would be grateful to hear from any copyright holder who is not here acknowledged and will undertake to rectify any errors or omissions in future editions of this book.

Contents

Citation Information

The chapters in this book were originally published in *World Futures*, volume 75, issue 1–2 (February 2019). When citing this material, please use the original page numbering for each article, as follows:

For any permission-related enquiries please visit:
http://www.tandfonline.com/page/help/permissions

Contributors

Jocelyn Chapman, PhD, is a transdisciplinarian with a special interest in cybernetics and systems thinking. She is the Director of the Transformative Inquiry Department at the California Institute of Integral Studies (CIIS) in San Francisco, USA. She also teaches in the online Transformative Leadership MA and Transformative Studies PhD programs at CIIS.

Bruce Clarke is the Paul Whitfield Horn Professor of Literature and Science in the Department of English at Texas Tech University, Lubbock, USA. His research focuses on 19th- and 20th-century literature and science, with special interests in systems theory, narrative theory, and ecology.

Frank Galuszka is a Professor Emeritus at the University of California Santa Cruz, USA. He taught at the University of the Arts, Philadelphia, USA; Vermont College of Norwich University, Montpelier, USA; and The Studio School of Painting and Sculpture, New York City, USA. From 1994 to 1999, he was the President of the *American Society for Cybernetics.*

Ray Ison is a Professor of Systems at The Open University, Milton Keynes, UK. His research and scholarship spans the biophysical and social, and is primarily interdisciplinary and collaborative.

Klaus Krippendorff is the Gregory Bateson Emeritus Professor of Communication at the University of Pennsylvania, Philadelphia, USA. His research focuses on the role of language and dialogue in the social construction of realities.

Paul Pangaro is a Professor of the Practice in the Human-Computer Interaction Institute at Carnegie Mellon University, Pittsburgh, USA. His research interests centre on the facilitation of conversation for new possibilities – between human and machine but also within an organization or team, or internal to an individual wanting to learn, collaborate, and act with clear, if evolving, intentions.

Lucas Pawlik is a Philosopher and Cyberneticist at the University of Vienna, Austria. He furthers the communication between scientific, educational, and business pioneers so that their cooperation creates stable socio-economic frameworks which help society to benefit from humanity's digitalization.

Bernard Scott is an independent academic. From 2016–2019 he was Gordon Pask Professor of Sociocybernetics at the International Center for Sociocybernetics Studies, Bonn, Germany. In 2010, he retired from Cranfield University, UK, as Reader in Cybernetics.

Peter D. Tuddenham is an organic philosopher, systems co-explorer, designer and creator, and ocean and earth literacy and knowledge architect. He cofounded the College of Exploration and is Past President of the International Society for the Systems Sciences (2018–2019).

INTRODUCTION

WHY CYBERNETICS? WHY LOVE?

JOCELYN CHAPMAN (iD)

Cyberneticians are an eclectic group, connected by their affinity for a way of seeing and knowing that is unfamiliar to most people—namely, one based on "the circularity of observing and communicating" (Von Foerster, 2003b, p. 289).[1] For those unversed in cybernetics, the term itself can seem cryptic. The range of definitions—most rather enigmatic—probably contributes to the obscurity of cybernetics today. At the same time, the definitions can be part of the allure of cybernetics. For example, Klaus Krippendorff (2008) proposed this enticing definition of cybernetics: "an inter-disciplinary discourse that brings forth radically reflexive realities" (p. 183).[2] Thomas Rid (2016) commented that "the word [cybernetics] refuses to be either noun or prefix. Its meaning is equally evasive, hazy and uncertain," and yet, "whatever it is, it is always stirring, it is always about the future, and it always has been" (p. xi). One way to learn more about how stirring cybernetics is, and how it might relate to the future, is through life stories of cyberneticians.

I have invited these authors to share their story regarding cybernetics so we might learn how they discovered cybernetics, how that discovery has influenced their work and lives, and what excites them about cybernetics. From these authors, we gain a greater sense of the richness and versatility of cybernetics as an approach to transdisciplinary inquiry. I believe "inquiring minds" is a trait that connects cyberneticians. Ranulph Glanville (2013) implied this when ruminating on the differences between cybernetics and systems thinkers: "Cybernetics seems to be more general, more philosophical, and more abstract than systems theory, which seems full of subdivisions, more pragmatic and more 'real world.' Perhaps cyberneticians are fascinated by questions whereas systemists like answers" (p. 47).[3] An extreme example of cyberneticians' high valuing of questions is found in Paul Pangaro's (2016) recent discussion of his "deep interest in creating a better-question engine" (p. 17) that could generate questions and then rank them for presentation to humans who would ultimately do the question selecting. For the love of good questions! Indeed, the personal narratives of these authors show an appreciation for interesting questions and transdisciplinary inquiry.

Cybernetics was transdisciplinary before the term "transdisciplinary" came into use.[4] While it was developed as a means of communication between experts in different disciplines, early developers' inquiry into "the nature of control" made cybernetics a way of seeing as well (Beer, 2002). In fact, Ranulph Glanville (2001) often referred to Margaret Mead's keynote paper, "The Cybernetics of Cybernetics," in which she describes cybernetics "as a way of looking at things and as a language for expressing what one sees" (1968, p. 2). And Mary Catherine Bateson (2001) stated more elaborately that, "Cybernetics can be a way of looking that cuts across fields, linking art and science and allowing us to move from a single organism to an ecosystem, from a forest to a university or a corporation, to recognize the essential recurrent patterns before taking action" (p. 87). She goes on to encourage us to view cybernetics as a unifying way of seeing the world, not as a tool to apply here and there. The authors in this collection show us many examples of what it's like to *see* cybernetically. Cybernetics is not their "area of interest"; it is how they think about what they do and it is their practice. As Ben Sweeting (2015) put it, the practice of cybernetics "consist[s] of the circular relation between how we act and how we explain or understand that action" (p. 1399). The cyberneticians gathered here reveal to us what it is like to think in terms of relationships and patterns that connect one relationship to another and what it is like, in practice, to "act to know."[5]

Why cybernetics? For one thing, "it is beautiful, it is human" (Glanville, 1995, p. 312). As humans, we are cognitive beings with the freedom and responsibility to choose our observing, our knowing, acting, and being, and that—all of that—is beautiful. Cybernetics is also an alternative to the dualistic and reductionistic paradigms that are dominant today and contribute to the complex crisis we are facing involving economics, poverty, climate change, environmental degradation, healthcare, surveillance and privacy, government accountability and transparency, migration, religious conflict, and more. We need to think differently about these messes.

As a participatory epistemology, cybernetics involves "acting to know" by recursively observing the effect of our actions and using this feedback to adjust our understanding and subsequent actions (Glanville, 2002; Keeney, 2005). The ethical significance of thinking cybernetically is found in the self-referential inclusion of the observer in their observing. Since we construct meanings, we are responsible for them and must respect this responsibility in others. "The logic of self-reference," Varela (1984) stated, "… should tell us that ethics—tolerance and pluralism, detachment from our own perceptions and values to allow for those of others—is the very foundation of knowledge, and also its final point" (p. 323). Cybernetics offers a relational, reflexive way of knowing in which the knower is responsible for their meaning-making, values, and ethics.

To inspire *World Futures*'s readers that are new to cybernetics and so those already enamored of cybernetics may hear our love songs in many keys, these authors were invited to respond to the prompt, "For the love of cybernetics," however they were moved or inspired by it.

NOTES

1. "Circularities" is often identified as the central notion of cybernetics, as discussed in Ranulph Glanville's (2011) "A (Cybernetic) Musing: Cybernetics and Circularities," and exemplified in Larry Richard's (2013) "Difference-Making From a Cybernetic Perspective: The Role of Listening and Its Circularities," and Joy Murray's (2006) "Cybernetic Circularity In Teaching and Learning."

2. More typical definitions of cybernetics refer to a "steersman" conducting error-correction to progress toward a goal (Heylighen & Joslin, 2001) or relating to observed systems and observing systems (Von Foerster, 1974). Larry Richards (2016) gave us "Cybernetics as a way of thinking about ways of thinking (of which it—cybernetics—is one)" (p. 48).

3. Of course, many will argue that cyberneticians are interested in solutions to "real world" problems, too. For example, in "What is Cybernetics?" Stafford Beer (2002) discusses not only the novelty of cybernetics, but its "relevance to what is called real-life" (p. 862).

4. Jean Piaget is credited with coining the term transdisciplinary in 1970, although the concerns giving rise to it were well established in the writings of mid-20th-century scholars (Bernstein, 2015).

5. "Act to know" is a reference to Heinz von Foerster's (2003a) well-known aesthetic imperative, "If you desire to see, learn how to act" (p. 227). This is used in developing an understanding of how learning occurs at a science museum in "Ethics and Aesthetics of Observing Frames" by Frederick Steier and Jane Jorgenson (2003).

ORCID

Jocelyn Chapman (iD) http://orcid.org/0000-0001-6561-8758

REFERENCES

Bateson, M. C. (2001). The wisdom of recognition. *Cybernetics & Human Knowing*, *8*(4), 87–90.

Beer, S. (2002). What is cybernetics? *Kybernetes*, *31*(2), 209–219. doi:10.1108/03684920210417283

Bernstein, J. H. (2015). Transdisciplinarity: A review of its origins, development, and current issues. *Journal of Research Practice*, *11*(1), 1.

Glanville, R. (1995). Chasing the blame. In:Research on progress—Advances in inter-disciplinary studies on systems research and cybernetics (Vol. 11, pp. 312–320). Ontario, Canada: Windsor.

Glanville, R. (2001). *Second order cybernetics (6.46. 3.3)*. Paper presented at the American Society for Cybernetics 2001 Conference, Vancouver, May.

Glanville, R. (2002). Doing the right thing: the problems of... Gerard de Zeeuw, academic guerilla. *Systems Research and Behavioral Science*, *19*(2), 107–113. doi:10.1002/sres.451

Glanville, R. (2011). A (cybernetic) musing: Cybernetics and circularities. *Cybernetics and Human Knowing*, *194*, 105–116.

Glanville, R. (2013). Cybernetics: Thinking through the technology. In D. Arnold (Ed.), *Traditions of systems theory: Major figures and contemporary developments* (pp. 45–77). New York, NY: Routledge.

Heylighen, F., & Joslin, C. (2001). Cybernetics and second-order cybernetics. In R. A. Meyers (Ed.), *Encyclopedia of physical science & technology*. New York, NY: Academic Press.

Keeney, B. (2005). Confessions of a cybernetic epistemologist. *Kybernetes*, *34*(3/4), 373–384. doi:10.1108/03684920510581558

Krippendorff, K. (2008). Cybernetics's reflexive turns. *Cybernetics and Human Knowing*, *15*(3–4), 173.

Mead, M. (1968). *Cybernetics of cybernetics*. Purposive systems: Proceedings of the First Annual Symposium of the American Society for Cybernetics. New York, NY: Spartan Books.

Murray, J. (2006). Cybernetic circularity in teaching and learning. *International Journal of Teaching and Learning in Higher Education*, *18*(3), 215–221.

Pangaro, P. (2016). Why do we want to live in cybernetics? *Cybernetics & Human Knowing*, *23*(2), 9–21.

Richards, L. (2013). Difference-making from a cybernetic perspective: The role of listening and its circularities. *Cybernetics & Human Knowing*, *20*(1–2), 59–68.

Richards, L. (2016). A history of the history of cybernetics: An agenda for an ever-changing present. *Cybernetics & Human Knowing*, *23*(1), 42–49.

Rid, T. (2016). *Rise of the machines: A cybernetic history*. New York, NY: WW Norton & Company.

Steier, F., & Jorgenson, J. (2003). Ethics and aesthetics of observing frames. *Cybernetics & Human Knowing*, *10*(3–4), 124–136.

Sweeting, B. (2015). Cybernetics of practice. *Kybernetes*, *44*(8/9), 1397–1405. doi: 10.1108/K-11-2014-0239

Varela, F. (1984). The creative circle: Sketches on the natural history of circularity. In P. Watzlavick (Ed.), *The invented reality* (pp. 309–324). New York, NY: W. W. Norton & Company.

Von Foerster, H. (1974). *Cybernetics of cybernetics: or, the control of control and the communication of communication*. Urbana-Champaign, IL: Biological Computer Laboratory.

Von Foerster, H. (2003a). On constructing a reality. In: *Understanding Understanding* (pp. 211–227). New York, NY: Springer.

Von Foerster, H. (2003b). *Ethics and second-order cybernetics Understanding understanding* (pp. 287–304). New York, NY: Springer.

TOWARD CYBER-SYSTEMIC THINKING IN PRACTICE

RAY ISON

This article is an invitation to be reflexive; reflexivity is a second-order process or reflection on reflection. The possibility that a reader might experience a reflexive moment is sought by avoiding a narrative trap: to believe the "coming to" of the issue title implies a state to arrive at, carefully planned, a purposeful journey, pursued by an enlightened individual devoid of all social relations. The author thus begins situated in a social system. Following Maturana, a social system is explained, as is what constitutes, or triggers, change, in a social system. An example of granting rivers sentience in law as an expansion of the social is explored

CHANGE IN A SOCIAL SYSTEM: CHANGE IN A STRUCTURE-DETERMINED SYSTEM

The title of this special edition and the espoused rationale are invitations that open up a reflexive space for an author who must imagine who a reader might be; it is an invitation to be reflexive on and in one's doings. Being reflexive is a second-order process such as reflection on reflection. The challenge in my doings is to create the possibility that a reader, reading, might also experience a reflexive moment. The desire for such a possibility is what I have come to term "taking a design turn." More about that later.

Framed as it is, participating in the generation of this special issue invites several modes of doing across different domains: doing history, autobiography, explaining, offering distinctions, seeking critical incidents and other domains, each of which might bring forth different accompanying emotionings (affection; fear; hubris; enthusiasm etc.). The trap I seek to avoid is the possibility that one develops a narrative as if the "coming to" of the issue title implies a state to be arrived at, or a carefully planned, purposeful journey, something pursued by an enlightened individual devoid of all social relations. For this reason, I begin by situating myself as within a social system. And in the spirit of Humberto Maturana, as much of my doing is, if I make that claim then I need to begin by offering an explanation for a social system and what might constitute change, or triggers for change, in a social system.

I have heard Maturana claim that before explaining a social system it is necessary to ask what is it that we experience when we claim we experience the social?[1] My understanding of his answer is that the social arises in the reciprocal experience of others arising as legitimate others in our living (i.e., the operation of the biology of love). Over and above structural drift in a culture, Maturana suggests that there are two main means by which more rapid changes in a social system may be triggered: (a) by encountering novel or "different" others that perturb one's established patterns of understanding as when traveling into new areas or countries and (b) moments of intense emotion in relationships where the desire for a future for the relationship is at stake—as with a spouse, lover, colleague, or friend. I am sure there are other "major change mechanisms" that operate, although the ones I wish to elaborate may be considered variants on these two (i.e., through):

- accepting or rejecting explanations;
- being open to differences that make a difference—the act of making a distinction in relation to one's self—which gives rise to experience; and
- avoiding persistent compromise in a relationship, thus maintaining enthusiasm and/or love.

I also want to make the point that the legitimate other who may arise through love may be another person but may also be another species or part of the biophysical world (what we mistakenly call "the environment"). From this perspective, the phenomena that give rise to the invention of terms such as Anthropocene, Econocene, or Capitalocene exemplify cyber-systemic breakdown and a failure of our social system in the sense I am using the term "social system" (Ison, Alexandra, & Wallis, 2018; Kunkel, 2017). But I do not want to start out in an emotion of fear or despair, although these easily arise in contemporary living (Bell, 2017).

In the Maturanan sense, because I am sitting, writing this article, it means that my organization as a human being continues to be conserved even though my structure has changed many times in my life to date (think of a tornado that exists as an organized dynamic of air particles, all of which are different at any moment in time; i.e., the structure is constantly changing). Yet I can also be understood as a structure-determined system: "A structure determined system is a system such that all that takes place in it, or happens to it at any instant, is determined by its structure at that instant. We living systems, as molecular systems, are structure determined systems" (Maturana n.d.). But as Maturana (n.d.) goes on to explicate: "the structure of a system is open to change, and can change in two ways:

1. structural changes through which the organization of the changing system is conserved; I shall call these changes of state [my example above of me as a human being]
2. structural changes through which the organization of the structurally changing system is lost, not conserved; I shall call these disintegrative changes" [e.g., death of an organism or "death" of a government]

In changes of state the operational characteristics of the system change while it conserves its class identity. In disintegrative changes, as the original system disappears, something else arises in its place.

Some clarification is called for at this point. If I accept the explanation that I can be understood as a structure-determined system, as I do, then no changes over my lifetime have been "caused" in the systematic or determinant sense by others or outside factors or forces. On the other hand, I have changed—an example of what Maturana describes as conservation of organization but changes in state (ibid). Stepping into a reflexive space I can choose to discern my life to date as operating in multiple domains with different elements and configurations; that is, as different systems (understood as epistemological heuristics rather than ontological entities). Whether these are best treated *as if* social systems is, however, another question because there is a big mismatch between what I, following Maturana, have claimed gives rise to a social system, and that which we use in every day speech to talk about the social, or a social system. A social scientist may claim that government X exemplified a social system, but on the basis of my claims here about what constitutes the social most governments would "fail the test" as to being a social system.

This introductory discourse on change is designed to explicate the methodological approach I have taken to this article. My coming to cybernetics has not been caused by any person or event. What is very clear to me are those moments of living in a conversational and praxis milieu in which the nature and trajectory of my structural coupling altered. Many of these were, of course, internal changes but always in response to perturbations brought about in particular relational dynamics including people, explanations, new distinctions, and thus experiences. The sample of moments and milieus that follow are not chronological and constitute a choice under the limitations of time and space. They convey, I hope, a cybernetic flavor.

RELATIONSHIP MAKING, MAINTAINING, AND BREAKING

Before departing this introductory narrative about change I want to connect to the work of Geoffrey Vickers (e.g., Vickers, 1965) and, via Checkland (e.g.,

Checkland, 1981, 1999; Checkland & Casar, 1986), to the work of C. West Churchman (1971). This lineage was explicated in illuminating detail by my colleague Chris Blackmore (2009). Vickers's idea that most speaks to me is the dynamic, systemic nature of what he calls cycles of appreciation that are constituted by choices (or non-choices) about relationship making, maintaining, and breaking. The design of inquiring systems, which, following Checkland (2002), I call "systemic inquiry" (Ison, 2017), is a way of framing what I am doing here. It is also what Chris and I have done, and invite our students to participate in, through our design of a core module in the Open University (OU) MSc in Systems Thinking in Practice called "Managing systemic change: Inquiry, action and interaction"d (Ison & Blackmore, 2014).

As I outlined in an editorial to a special edition of *Systems Research & Behavioral Science* that celebrated Vickers's work (Ison, 2005, p. 3), Sir Geoffrey's contribution was "to think and theorize about the processes of managing that he was involved in. He argued that managing was not an activity that could be quantified or rationalized or put into some algorithm, but always involved a very human ability to make judgments about the nature of situations, judgments about possible actions and their consequences, and judgments about values. ... These ideas went very much against the current orthodoxy, which was more concerned with determining efficient means of reaching pre-specified goals and emphasized the mathematical and quantitative aspects of planning."

What I find of value from Vickers's work is that through his own reflexivity he came to understand the primacy of relationship, a phenomenon that is recursive, reciprocal, and involving the key cybernetic notions espoused by Wiener (1948) of feedback (i.e., control or coordination) and communication even though Vickers did not express it in these terms. As I outlined, "at the core of his concerns was the question of 'relationship' which he characterized as the relationship between 'the forces which compose the system under observation, or between that system and its environment.' Vickers was working with systems thinking before the epistemological shift had occurred from 'hard' to 'soft'—from seeing systems as 'things' in the world rather than constructs used as epistemological devices (Checkland, 1999). My perception is that what attracted Vickers to Systems was the explanatory power of the intellectual field in relation to his own reflections on practice (Ison, 2005, p. 4).

I came to Vickers's writings from a background in plant-ecophysiology and agriculture. As an undergraduate my formal courses were, in conceptual terms, devoid of human beings as active subjects. Thus, when Vickers said, and I read: "Human Systems are Different" his work resonated with my own questioning of the ways in which science excluded social processes based on understandings of what it is to be human (Vickers 1972; 1973; 1983). Later, my colleague Richard Bawden and I wrote (Bawden & Ison, 1992):

> The work of Vickers (1983, 1984) is relevant to the activities of field-crop ecosystem researchers as members of organizations. Reviewing his life's work as a member of many organizations, Vickers (see Vickers, 1984; Checkland &

Casar, 1986) recognized that his actions were based on "an appreciative system" comprised of:

i.   a notion that the cycle of judgements and actions are organized as a system;

ii.   a separation of judgements about what is the case ("reality judgements") and judgements about what is good or bad, ("value judgements");

iii.   a concept of action judgements stemming from reality and value judgements;

iv.   an insistence on "relationship maintaining" as a richer concept of human action than the popular but poverty-stricken notion of goal seeking;

v.   a rich concept of day-to-day life as a flux of interacting events and ideas.

If an "appreciative system" such as Vickers's is adopted it follows that the "single problem-single answer" approach that scientists often bring to social issues is likely to be ineffective. (p. 30)

We were drawn to Vickers's work because of this latter phenomenon—the failure to see agriculture as a human activity and which made sense (to us) to see also as socially constructed. In his own way Vickers appreciated that we make and remake nature every day and thus must take responsibility for what we do. Much of my subsequent research has been concerned with the design of systemic processes to generate new understandings and practices in relation with the so-called "natural" world—for altering the "standards of fact and value" in terms of Vickers's appreciative system.

To summarize thus far: my coming to cybernetics has been markedly influenced by encountering intellectual lineages in which my own particular traditions of understanding are lived and conserved (Russell & Ison, 1993). The main three I have highlighted thus far as relevant to my history are: (a) Maturana and the biology of love; (b) Churchman and Checkland for the design of inquiring systems' and (c) Vickers's understandings of appreciation based on relationship (plus his reflexive praxis). The milieu in which these explanations became relevant to me was that of a small agricultural college, Hawkesbury Agricultural College, on the outskirts of Sydney, Australia where I accepted my first post-PhD academic post in 1982 (see Bawden & Packham, 1993).

BEING OPEN TO EXPERIENCE

A Creative Intellectual Milieu at the Margins

Within the Hawkesbury milieu I first became aware of the different lineages that had evolved in relation to systems and cybernetics as exemplified through societies such as the American Society for Cybernetics (ASC), the

International Society for the Systems Sciences, and the Systems Dynamics Society. Aware, much later, that this institutional complexity was constraining the overall intellectual field I combined with Gary Boyd at an ASC meeting at Renasselaer Polytechnic, Troy NY in July 2010 to argue the case for reconsidering the field as cyber-systemics (see also Boyd & Zeman, 2007; Ison, 2016a).[2] I have tried to hold to this position ever since and will do so now in the remainder of the article.

My long-term friend and collaborator David Russell was the first to introduce me to cybernetics in a manner that was, and remains, invitational. On Friday, May 9, 1986, David hosted a workshop at Hawkesbury to explore the work he had done while on a sabbatical leave; the paper he wrote that formed the basis of our discussions, "How we see the world determines what we do in the world: Preparing the ground for action research," remains as relevant today as I found it then. We have marked over 30 years of collaboration with the publication "Fruits of Gregory Bateson's epistemological crisis: Embodied mind-making and interactive experience in research and professional praxis" (Russell & Ison, 2017) in a special edition of the *Canadian Journal of Communication* on the theme: "At the Margins of Cybernetics" (Theophanidis, Thibault, & Trudel, 2017). It was with David and another colleague, and Maturana scholar (Lloyd Fell),[3] that I attended my first Maturana workshop in Melbourne in 1993. Maturana's work became, and has remained, relevant to much that I do under the rubric of cyber-systemics.

Intersections With Systemic Family Therapy

Soon after I began my collaboration with David, my partner, Cathy Humphreys, began a PhD in social work; the thesis (*Child sexual assault disclosure: Mothers in crisis*) drew on cybernetic understandings, as they had then been applied within systemic family therapy, as well as feminist post-structuralism (Humphreys, 1991). Having been invited to help with reading and commenting on chapters, especially those related to systemic family therapy, I had an opportunity that can be understood in terms of relationship maintaining and/or love, to meaningfully engage with the cybernetic literature that my partner was able to synthesize. It was thus pleasing for me, nearly 20 years later, to discover that my book *Systems practice: How to act in a climate change world* (Ison, 2010) had been taken up and used in the marriage and family therapy doctoral program run by the University of Louisiana at Monroe (e.g., McClendon, 2016).

Humphreys (1991) argued that the experience of mothers in her study was "explained most clearly by looking first through the lens of second order cybernetics ... and then ideas from post-structuralism" (p. 246). The second-order cybernetic principles that most extended "understanding of mothers of sexually abused children were perception, the individual in context, ... recursion, orders of recursion and the principle of circular causality" (p. 247). Humphreys (1991), like many other feminist theorists and, more recently international development practitioners and theorists (e.g., Green, 2016), went on to argue that second-order cybernetics "failed to develop an adequate explanation for the exercise and mechanism of power" (p. 283). My own understanding then and now was that this scholarship represents a misreading of power within the second-order tradition. Attending to this issue, which is persistent, I have, in the second edition of my book (Ison, 2017), argued that incipient cyber-systems practitioners might be advised to: "name power as part of all that [they] do if [they] think naming it helps [their] praxis; remember[-ing] that ... reflexive systems praxis has the potential to reconfigure relational dynamics in situations of concern and is thus a praxis that can 'undo' configurations, dispositions and discourses of power" (p. 340).

Enthusiasm as Theory, Biological Driving Force, and Methodology

In several publications, I have accounted through reflexive stories, my arriving in cybernetics as an embodied knower mainly over the period 1989–1994 (Ison and Russell 2000a, 2000b, 2007; Russell & Ison 2004, 2005). This was a particularly rich and rewarding period both personally and professionally and included my move from the University of Sydney to The Open University (UK) at the end of 1993. My first story relates experiences I had in the early 1980s of development failure set primarily in Tanzania and my conclusion that the failure was best explained in terms of the misplaced understandings of the would-be developers (Ison & Russell, 2000a). The second story relates the context in which the concept of enthusiasm became meaningful to me as part of my collaboration with David Russell within the Hawkesbury milieu (Russell & Ison, 2000); the third is how we built a research project around enthusiasm to replace the dominant information or technology transfer model of doing Research & Development (R&D).

Perhaps most significantly, our understanding of enthusiasm (from the Greek, *en theos*, meaning "the god within") that we elucidated through our co-research with pastoralists as an alternative basis for doing R&D (Community Approaches to Rangelands Research [CARR], 1993; Russell & Ison, 2000) has stood the test of time in my own praxis; trusting the emotion of enthusiasm as the motivational driver of relationship has been central to my praxis since this time. We also found that hegemonic and imposed models or programs that enforce consensus, or compromise, militate against personal enthusiasm and that enthusiasm must be bounded through collective responsibility, transparency, and rituals that create a sense of common purpose. We established that enthusiasm could be understood and used as (a) an intellectual or theoretical notion; (b) an emotion or driving force; and (c) methodology underpinned by use of narrative (see Russell & Ison, 2000, 2017). Maturana and Bateson and others within the second-order cybernetic tradition provided inspiration for our work (Russell & Ison, 2017). In our CARR project (CARR, 1993) and in subsequent research and praxis situations we have each found our praxis approach based on enthusiasm robust for designing and doing R&D, undertaking academic practice and valuable for process designs in uncertain, multiperspective, multistakeholder situations (e.g., Ison, 2016b).

Subsequent stories that have not been told in any systematic manner include how my understandings from our elucidation of enthusiasm was used to "facilitate" a process of organizational change in my own university (e.g., Armson & Ison, 2001; Ison & Armson, 2006), to contribute to the design of a process consultancy in South Africa in 1994 (Cousins, 1994) and in reconceptualizing, in cyber-systemic terms, staff induction (Armson, Ison, Short, Ramage, & Reynolds, 2001), and other forms of practice (e.g., scenarioing; Ison, Grant, & Bawden, 2014).

Toward Cyber-Systemic Governing

As one who has long held that it is ethical to "walk-one's-talk" much of my scholarly praxis in the period 1995 to the present has been within my own university in a series of systemic action research projects (see Armson, 2011) and/ or in settings concerned with the co-evolutionary governance of situations usefully framed as structurally coupled social–biophysical systems such as river catchments or watersheds (Colvin et al., 2014; Ison et al., 2018). The latter has been conducted in recent years under the rubric of cyber-systemic governing in the Anthropocene (see Ison 2016a; Ison & Schlindwein, 2015; http://www.open.ac.uk/blogs/govan/). At the core of this scholarship are two key cybernetic understandings:

1. governance, or more accurately governing, is a praxis that I frame in the following terms (Ison et al., 2018, pp. 1212–1213):

   Little recent scholarship about governance retains the integrity of its etymological roots—the Greek verb *kubernao,* meaning to steer. Ampere (1834) drew on this understanding to formulate the science of civil government (see Tsien, 1954). From these roots Wiener (1948) reformulated the term cybernetics, which unfortunately became conserved as a noun rather than a verb. By drawing upon the intellectual lineage of cyber-systemics ... we frame governance using the central metaphor of a helmsperson (sailor) steering, or charting a viable course in response to feedback (from currents, wind) in relation to purposes that are renegotiated within an unfolding context—that is, in repeatedly recalibrated responses to uncertainty. The dynamics, between social and biophysical systems are mediated by artefactual technologies—such as the boat—and social technologies—like the rules of a sailing race. ... From this metaphor we take the term "cyber-systemic governance." We avoid the idea that purpose, or goals, are pre-given preferring instead the idea that "purpose elaborating" is integral to governing, rather than the narrower idea of goal seeking. (Checkland, 1985)

2. articulating and developing a cyber-systemic praxeology capable, when enacted, institutionalized, invested in, of making a significant contribution to maintaining a viable structural coupling of humans

with the biosphere (i.e., cyber-systemic governing). To succeed I would claim we humans need to recover, or rediscover, our cyber-systemic sensibilities, become more cyber-systemically literate and build quickly a cadre of citizens and professionals able to do cyber-systemic thinking in practice. (Ison & Shelley, 2016; Reynolds, Shah, Wedlock, Ison, & Blackmore, 2016)

LIVING AND CONSERVING CYBER-SYSTEMIC THINKING IN PRACTICE

Maturana's invitation to consider the question: What do we do when we do what we do? has, since I first experienced the invitation, guided much of my own doing. This is the organizing question in Ison (2010; 2017) and the OU MSc module described earlier. It is also the question that will underpin a new book currently under preparation with colleague Ed Straw concerning what we do when we claim to be doing governing. For anyone with cyber-systemic sensibilities it is readily apparent that our "governance systems" are no longer fit for purpose. It would be good if in reinventing what we do, cyber-systemic understandings and practices could come to the fore. So, my invitation to you dear reader is to do what you can to bring this transformation about. Unfortunately, the prevailing paradigm, what Donald Schön (1995) described as technical rationality, is pervasive and persistent. The place to start, I would suggest, is with our own practice and, through acting with cyber-systemic awareness and literacy, influencing the process designs and institutions (as in norms, rules of the human game) within which we must function (Ison, 2017).

As an example, let me conclude by drawing attention to recent institutional innovations with potential to shift the governance of rivers by reframing them as social systems as outlined above.[4] New Zealand's lawmakers have recently granted a river the legal rights of a human; a parliamentary vote has ensured "the roughly 90-mile Whanganui River will be represented by two guardians in legal matters that concern the waterway. The legislation marks a monumental victory for the local Māori people, who view the river as 'an indivisible and living whole ... '" (http://n.pr/2qi1dbb). Just as a court of human rights, a particular institution, was sought by its designers to enhance the social, with appropriate changes/designs it is possible to admit "others as legitimate others" into the social. The challenge for future cyber-systemists is to invent new institutions, governing frameworks and praxis that perturbs the structural drift of our current "governance systems" and thus opens up new trajectories for our future living.

ACKNOWLEDGMENTS

I extend my thanks to all collaborators past and present; my particular thanks to Pille Bunnell for her insightful contributions to the development of my book (Ison, 2010), to Ranulph Glanville for enabling me to experience the poetry of cybernetics, and to Jocelyn Chapman for the invitation to contribute.

NOTES

1. Colloquium on Autopoiesis & Social Systems, London School of Economics, May 11–12, 1998. "In what sense can social systems be seen as autopoietic?"
2. See http://www.asc-cybernetics.org/2010/wp-content/uploads/2010/08/GaryBoyd.pdf and http://www.asc-cybernetics.org/2010/wp-content/uploads/2010/08/RayIson.pdf
3. http://www.pnc.com.au/~lfell/
4. The example material draws on Geoff Lawtoon, http://bit.ly/2pKSkXC

REFERENCES

Armson, R. (2011). *Growing wings on the way. Systems thinking for messy situations.* Exeter, UK: Triarchy Press.

Armson, R., & Ison, R. L. (2001). If you're a fish what can you know about the water? Some reflections on doing Systems when you are immersed in the context. Conference of the American Society of Cybernetics, Vancouver, May 2001.

Armson, R., Ison, R. L., Short, L., Ramage, M., & Reynolds, M. (2001). Rapid institutional appraisal (RIA): A systemic approach to staff development. *Systemic Practice and Action Research, 14,* 763–777. doi:10.1023/A:1013182429327

Bawden, R. J., & Ison, R. L. (1992). The purpose of field-crop ecosystems: Social and economic aspects. In C. J. Pearson (Ed.), *Field-crop ecosystems* (pp. 11–35). Amsterdam, the Netherlands: Elsevier.

Bawden, R. J., & Packham, R. G. (1993). Systemic praxis in the education of the agricultural systems practitioner. *Systems Practice, 6* (1), 7–19. doi:10.1007/BF01059677

Bell, S. (2017). *Formations of terror.* Cambridge: Cambridge Scholars Publishing.

Blackmore, C. P. (2009). Learning systems and communities of practice for environmental decision making (PhD Thesis). The Open University, Milton Keynes, UK.

Boyd, G., & Zeman, V. (2007). Designing cybersystemically for symviability. *Kybernetes, 36* (9/10), 1255–1265. doi:10.1108/03684920710827274

Checkland, P. (1981). *Systems thinking, systems practice.* Chichester, UK: Wiley.

Checkland, P. B. (1985). From optimizing to learning: A development of systems thinking for the 1990s. *Journal of the Operational Research Society, 26,* 757–767. doi:10.2307/2582164

Checkland, P. (1999). *SSM: A 30 years retrospective.* Chichester, UK: Wiley

Checkland, P. (2002). The role of the practitioner in a soft systems study, Quarterly Newsletter of the Open University Systems Society (OUSyS). Open University: Milton Keynes, No. 27, March 2002, pp. S5–S11

Checkland, P., & Casar, A. (1986). Vickers' concept of an appreciative system: A systemic account. *Journal of Applied Systems Analysis, 13,* 3–17.

Churchman, C. W. (1971). *The design of inquiring systems: Basic concepts of systems and organizations.* New York, NY: Basic Books.

Colvin, J., Blackmore, C., Chimbuya, S., Collins, K. B., Dent, M., Goss, J., ... Seddaiu, G. (2014). In search of systemic innovation for sustainable development: A design praxis emerging from a decade of social learning inquiry. *Research Policy, 43*(4), 760–771. doi:10.1016/j.respol.2013.12.010

Community Approaches to Rangelands Research (CARR). (1993). Marketing of Middle Micron Wool. Researching with people on issues that make a difference. Monograph. University of Sydney & University of Western Sydney. 44 pp.

Cousins, B. ed. (1994). Issues and options for institutional change for rural development, agriculture and land reform. Summary and Overview. Policy Paper 9, Land & Agriculture Policy Centre, Johannesburg. 69 pp.

Green, D. (2016). *How change happens.* Oxford, UK: Oxford University Press.

Humphreys, C. (1991). *Child sexual assault disclosure: Mothers in crisis* (PhD dissertation). Sydney, Australia: University of N.S.W.

Ison, R. L. (2005). Editorial. Geoffrey Vickers 2004: Contemporary applications and changing appreciative settings. *Special Edition Systems Research & Behavioral Science, 22*, 1–8. doi:10.1002/sres.691

Ison, R. L. (2010). *Systems practice: how to act in a climate-change world.* London, UK: Springer and The Open University.

Ison, R. L. (2016a). Governing in the Anthropocene: What future systems thinking in practice? *Systems Research and Behavioral Science, 33*(5), 595–613. doi:10.1002/sres.2421

Ison, R. L. (2016b). Transforming nature-society relations through innovations in research praxis: A coevolutionary systems approach, In B. Hubert & N. Mathieu (Eds.), *Interdisciplinarités entre Natures et Sociétés: Colloque de Cerisy. EcoPolis* (Vol 26., pp. 47–70). Brussels, Belgium: Peter Lang.

Ison, R. L. (2017). *Systems practice: how to Act. In situations of uncertainty and complexity in a climate-change world.* (2nd ed.,) London, UK: Springer and The Open University.

Ison, R. L., & Russell, D. B. (2000a). Exploring some distinctions for the design of learning systems. *Cybernetics and Human Knowing, 7*(4), 43–56.

Ison, R. L., & Russell, D. B. eds. (2000b). *Agricultural extension and rural development: Breaking out of traditions.* Cambridge, UK: Cambridge University Press, 239 p.

Ison, R. L., & Armson, R. (2006). Think, act & play im Leadership der Kybernetik zweiter Ordnung. Lernende Organisation, pp. 12–23. Zeitschrift fur systemishes Management und Organisation No 33, September/Oktober (www.lo.isct.net) ISSN 1609-1248.

Ison, R. L., & Russell, D. B. eds. (2007). *Agricultural extension and rural development: Breaking out of knowledge transfer traditions.* Paperback. Cambridge, UK: Cambridge University Press. 239 p.

Ison, R. L., & Blackmore, C. (2014). Designing and developing a reflexive learning system for managing systemic change. *Systems, 2*(2), 119–136.) doi:10.3390/systems2020119

Ison, R. L., & Schlindwein, S. (2015). Navigating through an 'ecological desert and a sociological hell': A cyber-systemic governance approach for the Anthropocene. *Kybernetes, 44*(6/7), 891–902. doi:10.1108/K-01-2015-0007

Ison, R. L., & Shelley, M. (2016). Governing in the anthropocene: Contributions from systems thinking in practice? ISSS yearbook special issue. *Systems Research and Behavioral Science, 33*(5), 589–594. doi:10.1002/sres.2436

Ison, R. L., Grant, A., & Bawden, R. B. (2014). Scenario praxis for systemic and adaptive governance: A critical framework. *Environment and Planning C: Government and Policy, 32*(4), 623–640. doi:10.1068/c11327

Ison, R. L., Alexandra, J., & Wallis, P. J. (2018). Governing in the Anthropocene: Cyber-systemic antidotes to the malaise of modern governance. *Sustainability Science, 13*(5), 1209–1223. doi:10.1007/s11625-018-0570-5

Kunkel, B. (2017). The capitalocence. *The London Review of Books, 39*(5), 22–28.

Maturana, H. (n.d.). *Autopoiesis, structural coupling and cognition.* http://www.isss. org/maturana.htm (Accessed 14th May 2017).

McClendon, K. S. (2016). *Not power but beauty: How systemic sensing and engaging inspire therapeutic change* (PhD Dissertation). University of Louisiana at Monroe, Department of Educational Leadership and Counseling (Marriage and Family Therapy), May.

Reynolds, M., Shah, R., Wedlock, E., Ison, R., & Blackmore, C. (2016). Enhancing Systems Thinking in Practice at the Workplace: eSTEeM final report. The OU Centre for STEM Pedagogy.

Russell, D. B., & Ison, R. L. (1993). The research-development relationship in rangelands: An opportunity for contextual science. Invited Plenary Paper, Proc. IVth International Rangeland Congress, Montpellier, 1991. Vol. 3, pp. 1047–1054.

Russell, D. B., & Ison, R. L. (2000). Enthusiasm: Developing critical action for second-order R&D. In R. L. Ison & D. B. Russell (Eds.), *Agricultural extension and rural development: Breaking out of traditions* (pp. 136–160). Cambridge, UK: Cambridge University Press.

Russell, D. B., & Ison, R. L. (2004). Maturana's intellectual contribution as a choreography of conversation and action. *Cybernetics & Human Knowing, 11*(2), 36–48.

Russell, D. B., & Ison, R. L. (2005). The researcher of human systems is both choreographer and chorographer. *Systems Research and Behavioral Science, 22*(2), 131–138. doi:10.1002/sres.680

Russell, D. B., & Ison, R. L. (2017). Fruits of Gregory Bateson's epistemological crisis: Embodied mind-making and interactive experience in research and professional praxis. *Canadian Journal of Communication, 42* (3), 485–514. doi:10.22230/ cjc.2017v42n3a3194

Schön, D. A. (1995). Knowing-in-action: The new scholarship requires a new epistemology, Change, November/December, 27–34.

Theophanidis, P., Thibault, G., & Trudel, D. (2017). Guest editorial. At the margins of cybernetics. *Canadian Journal of Communication, 42*, 397–405. doi:10.22230/ cjc.2017v42n3a3304

Tsien, H. S. (1954). *Engineering cybernetics, preface viii.* New York, NY: McGraw Hill.

Vickers, G. (1965). *The art of judgement.* London, UK: Chapman and Hall (Republished by Harper and Row, 1983 and Sage, 1995).

Vickers, G. (1972). *Freedom in a rocking boat.* Harmondsworth, UK: Penguin.

Vickers, G. (1973). *Making institutions work.* New York, NY: Wiley.

Vickers, G. (1983). *Human systems are different.* New York, NY: Harper & Row.

Vickers, G. (1984). *Human systems are different.* London, UK: Harper & Row.

Wiener, N. (1948). *Cybernetics: Or control and communication in the animal and the machine.* Cambridge, MA: MIT Press.

FINDING CYBERNETICS

BRUCE CLARKE

At mid-career as a tenured professor of modern literature, I finally found cybernetics. It was a slow-rolling revelation, a protracted unraveling, for it took me quite a while to unwrap cybernetics' conceptual core from out of the layers of adjacent or covering discourses that had obscured or forgotten their own origins in the fecundity of cybernetic ideas. Heinz von Foerster's relation to the *Whole Earth Catalog* and the systems counterculture around *CoEvolution Quarterly* were instrumental for my subsequent cybernetic development toward the work of Maturana, Varela, and Luhmann on the one hand, and Lovelock and Margulis on the other.

My graduate work in the English department at SUNY/Buffalo pursued traditional period studies—Romanticism and modernism—in a standard national specialization—British literature. This profile reflected only my own desire at the time for training in the standard canon. Buffalo's graduate literature program, meanwhile, had emerged from the late sixties streamlined, shorn of lengthy distributions of required courses, and wide open to independent and interdisciplinary studies. By 1974, the year I arrived, it had entered a gloriously radical non-canonical phase. One proceeded right past the MA degree to do doctoral study almost from the get-go. Two seminars plus the composition discussion group pieced out one's semester schedule. After a minimum of seven seminars you could form an exploratory committee and set to work on a dissertation project. At the time, I did not fully appreciate that I had stumbled my way out of a meandering college experience into graduate-school heaven.

Moreover, especially due to its heady program in comparative literature, Buffalo in the seventies had become a top venue for the study of high theory—poststructuralism, Lacanian and other post-Freudian schools of psychoanalysis, and deconstruction. The transgressive historian Michel Foucault had visited in the sixties. The inventor of deconstruction, philosopher Jacques Derrida, visited during my time. I sat in a packed classroom listening to him lecture in French, not grasping a word. Still, one could not but participate in the aura. The professors I worked with were not ultra–high theory types but were none-theless cut to the Buffalo mold of "literature and." That's why I had applied there, attracted to its programs in literature and psychology and literature and philosophy. Alongside Wordsworth, Coleridge, Keats, and D. H. Lawrence, I studied Kant's *Critique of Judgment*, Hegel's *Phenomenology of Mind*, and large swaths of Freud's collected works. A decade later, I was flush with aca-demic tenure but getting restless in my standard academic field, when news of an organized specialization in literature and science came over my horizon, offering the prospect of a kind of intellectual homecoming to my graduate roots in do-it-yourself interdisciplinarity.

I can date the onset of my transition from amorphous Romanticist to literary systems theorist to a precise moment in 1987 that set into motion a series of professional decisions confirming me in this new direction. I can also specify the texts that initiated and guided my path toward cybernetics writ large. Looking back over the works on this transitional shelf, I note that cybernetic conceptuality was present there, but mostly in spirit. The letter of cybernetics was largely on the margins, or, to put it more brutally, in a state of marginal-ization. Instead, front and center in these works was the it-discourse of that moment, chaos theory, technically termed dynamical systems theory. Its vehicle was James Gleick's (1987) popular-science bombshell, *Chaos: Making a New Science*. In Washington, D.C. attending an academic conference that year, walking around Dupont Circle I happened to pass a bookstore with prom-inently piled stacks of *Chaos* in their display case. I do not recall that I had any prior awareness of this work, but for whatever reason, something clicked with Gleick. I walked in and purchased a copy. Soon I was hopelessly hooked.

Chaos was a fateful first significant encounter with multiple dialects of sys-tems theory. It was not just the appeal of "chaos" and "turbulence" to a mind steeped in Romantic imagery. It was also the conceptual appeal of scientific-ally vetted notions of "nonlinearity" and "unpredictability." Add to that the esthetic lures of fractal-geometric images, the fortuitous butterfly shape of the Lorenz attractor, the jagged mathematical appeal of the Koch curve, the self-similar infinities of the Mandelbrot set. Looking back now on this text one may also note, pulsing quietly in the background, propping up the chaos-theor-etical ferment, the cybernetic motherlode of circular operations. Positive and negative feedbacks supported functional iteration in population modeling; com-putational recursion produced self-similarity in fractal forms. *Chaos* took both modes of looping cycles entirely for granted, with no gloss on their cybernetic pedigrees. Indeed, although the shadow of cybernetics falls all over chaos the-ory, the word "cybernetics" is scant in this text and absent from its index.

However, what *Chaos* does explicitly draw out for discussion is cybernet-ics' frequent partner or fraternal twin, the information theory of Claude Shannon (Shannon & Weaver, 1949). The chapter "The Dynamical Systems Collective" begins by evoking what a discerning eye may note as a surviving remnant of the California systems counterculture. Cybernetic hero Gregory Bateson is mentioned in passing as one of the intellectual luminaries drawing the "mix of bright nonconformists attracted to Santa Cruz" who were "influenced by the free-thinking ideology of the time" (Gleick, 1987, p. 243). With this preposterously anachronistic journalistic cliché Gleick managed to sweep away the wider legacy of the American counterculture, in particular the Whole Earth movement as well as its profound grounding in cybernetic ideas—as if UC/Santa Cruz in 1977 had no significant connection to Stewart Brand's Sausalito just up the coast, no ties to the alternative life- and thought-styles, whole systems and ecological thinking disseminated therefrom, as if the intellectual refinements of the late sixties abroad in the mid-seventies had been a long lifetime and not a mere decade prior to the mid-eighties moment of his writing. One senses in the ignoring or dismissal of these links a snippet of the pervasive amnesia in the revisionary histories of the Reagan era. Like Jimmy Carter's solar panels ripped off the White House roof, much of the cultural saga of cybernetics has also been discarded by various regressive regimes, "ideologies of the time" rather less "free-thinking."

I will come back later to the systems counterculture. As we learn, the "Dynamical Systems Collective," aka the "Chaos Cabal," consisted of a handful of brilliant graduate students in the Santa Cruz physics department who put the completion of their safely mainstream dissertations on extended hold to go off the disciplinary map and explore the virtual world of computer-generated images of strange attractors—mathematical systems of nonlinear equations simulating the potentially chaotic behaviors of actual dynamical systems. These young nonconformists centered their attention on systemic details previously considered marginal issues of error and insufficient precision to be excluded from a physics based on an ideal of determinability. Their intellectual lure was the discovery of modes of order within seemingly disorderly systems, systemic forms of disorderly order not entirely random and yet not entirely predictable. Chaos cabalist Doyne Farmer is quoted as commenting: "The system is deterministic, but you can't say what it's going to do next. ... I always felt that the spontaneous emergence of self-organization ought to be a part of physics" (Gleick, 1987, pp. 251–252).

Chaos again omits to note that the dialect of their quest for an analytical language capable of describing the constrained chaos of these dynamical systems is classically cybernetic. Heinz von Foerster's "On Self-Organizing Systems and their Environments" was published a generation earlier (von Foerster, 1960; see also Clarke, 2009a). Typical of cybernetic discussion in its first decades, his paper is suffused with the discourse of information theory, applied in this instance to a series of thought experiments concerning the possible ordering effects of seeming randomness, or "noise," on "self-organizing systems." Farmer's emphasis on the unpredictability of complex systems could also plausibly be tinged with a discursive development nearly contemporary with the coalescence of the Dynamical Systems Collective, the second-order cybernetics of von Foerster's "non-trivial machines" (for a summary discussion, see von Foerster & Poerksen, 2002, pp. 54–61). In other words, von Foerster and his colleagues were thinking in terms of what came to be called chaos theory both concurrently and *avant la lettre*.

Gleick's (1987) narrative continues: "The most characteristically Santa Cruzian input on chaos research involved a piece of mathematics cum philosophy known as information theory" (p. 255). Gleick's exposition thereof does enable a non-specialist reader to grasp the scientific innovations of the Chaos Cabal in some detail. It was certainly my first primer on the topic, and it excited me on several levels. One was simply the seeming proximity of "information" to my own stock in trade as a scholar of discourse and its interpretation. But another was the conceptual glamor of a term Shannon introduced into information theory—*entropy*, which names the tendency of the energy within closed physical systems to dissipate or become disordered, to level off at thermodynamic equilibrium, and thus become unavailable for further work. Gleick rightly notes how Shannon's whimsical coinage of *message* "entropy" as a probabilistic quantitative measure of informatic value seemed to many to endow his mathematical theory of communication with universal connotations. Information as "entropy"—that is, as measured relative to the (dis)order and (un)predictability of the messages transmitted over communication systems—could now bid to be treated as a physical entity on a par with matter and energy.

I fell in with the informatic program wholeheartedly, especially as it seemed to fill the entire horizon of discussion at that time. The specialization of literature and science and the popularization of chaos theory both arose in the later 1980s, a moment when the legacy of cybernetics per se was in some eclipse while its twin discourse information theory enjoyed increasing salience with the rise of the personal computer, social media, and the Internet. The American scholar of French literature and philosophy William R. Paulson published *The Noise of Culture: Literary Texts in a World of Information* (Paulson 1988). Fresh from the world according to *Chaos*, I zeroed in on its chapter "Self-Organizing Systems: Information and Noise." Paulson's text repaired some of the lacunae in Gleick's treatment with a short but pointed section citing von Foerster's (1960) paper in the context of the longer cybernetic interest in the concept of self-organization as a general, potentially computational description of the phenomenon of entropy-reduction in living systems. This may well have been my first infusion of specifically cybernetic references. But Paulson's interests were primarily information-theoretic: he elicited the French theoretical biologist Henri Atlan's development of von Foerster's suggestions concerning "self-organization from noise" for a theory of biological form (Atlan, 1972), but focused most pervasively on the major uptake of Atlan's biological informatics in the work of the French philosopher of science Michel Serres (see Serres, 1982).

In *Neocybernetics and Narrative* I have described the impact Serres's work had on me and my immediate colleagues as we were gearing up to do literature and science:

> Serres is among the first humanistic expositors at the intersection of information theory and postmodern discourse, and I think, still among the best. Two key

articles working this broadly cybernetic terrain are "Platonic Dialogue" and "The Origin of Language: Biology, Information Theory, and Thermodynamics," side-by-side chapters of the 1982 volume *Hermes: Literature, Science, Philosophy*. For more than a decade, this text was the main source of Anglophone appreciation of Serres's work. Thus, it entered deeply into the tissue of his American reception, my own included. Serres elegantly captures key elements of information theory and efficiently conveys them so as to pervade ensuing critical discourses engaged with cybernetics, self-organization, chaos and complexity theories, actor-network theory, emergence, and the like. (Clarke, 2014b, 58)

But with a bit of distance and some exposure to other varieties of systems theory, one may now conclude that in their bid for universal application, Serres's avid adaptations of Atlan's biological informatics literally do not hold water. That is, they cannot provide an account for the formal and operational autonomy of living beings. With Serres, to oversimplify, form is sacrificed to the stochastic vagaries of noise (see Clarke, 2014b, pp. 56–73). I argue instead that when the systemic organizations under discussion are more properly described as autopoietic or cognitive, one needs to move beyond strained analogies to informatic transmission or data processing. In short, if one places a premium on the viable self-maintenance of self-referential systems—such as organic bodies, which are operationally closed or self-binding, even while environmentally and thermodynamically open—one will prefer second-order (or neo-) cybernetic descriptions.

Nonetheless, it took me another decade to complete that transfer of theoretical allegiance. Throughout the nineties, I was besotted with entropy, thermodynamic and informatic, topics that I prepared for literary application through the discourse of allegory. The primary text inspiring this phase of my research was *Chaos Bound: Orderly Disorder in Contemporary Literature and Science* (Hayles, 1990). Whereas *The Noise of Culture* briefly acknowledged von Foerster as cybernetic context for Atlan's biosystemic application of information theory, *Chaos Bound* echoed Gleick in foregrounding the discourse of information while omitting to index "cybernetics." Yet this is a work that features discussions of feedback, recursion, control, observation, self-organization, Norbert Wiener, Stanislaw Lem's *The Cyberiad: Fables for the Cybernetic Age* (Lem 1985), and, at the beginning of the chapter on "Chaos and Poststructuralism," a footnote acknowledging an otherwise unspecified indebtedness "to Bateson's illuminating analyses of communication dialectics" in *Steps to an Ecology of Mind* (Bateson, 1972; Hayles, 1990, p. 176n1). Admittedly, these quibbles emerge only in hindsight. At the time, although I was not yet ready to acknowledge the validity of Hayles's critique of Serres's theoretical excesses, I was fully drawn in by her chapter "Self-Reflexive Metaphors in Maxwell's Demon and Shannon's Choice: Finding the Passages" (Hayles, 1990, pp. 31–60).

It was the Demon that particularly captured my imagination. Maxwell's Demon infused literary repercussions into the scientific discourse of thermodynamic entropy. Considered generically and in their classical provenance, demons or daemons are allegorical beings, symbolic bearers and vehicles of doctrinal (philosophical or theological) meanings. The allegory of thermodynamics in Maxwell's Demon "occupies the slim margin of escape Kelvin left open when he said that heat death is inevitable if man remains 'as at present constituted.' ... Like guardians of portals to other realms in ancient myths, the Demon is a liminal figure who stands at a threshold that separates not just slow molecules from fast but an ordered world of will from the disordered world of chaos" (Hayles, 1990, p. 43). Hayles then traced how the figure of Maxwell's Demon as an order-producing agent reemerged, in the aftermath of Shannon's evocation of entropy in information theory, as a mobile avatar for the possibility of overcoming the dissipation of *information* by some willful recovery or reproduction of systemic order.

I have already suggested that, as channeled through *L'Organisation biologique et la théorie de l'information*, von Foerster's "On Self-Organizing Systems and their Environments" provided the original template for the treatment of the Demon as an *observer* of systems, an observer that can be located both within and without a given system, on either side of a systemic boundary.[1] Hayles treats the Demon's mobile positionality as a "self-reflexive metaphor," a sort of personification of the information-theoretic concept of *equivocation* operating through a form of doubling or mirror-reversal. Posited as an observer of informatic traffic—or in von Foerster's idiom, as an observing system in its own right—such a cognitive agent can then create "surplus meaning" by adding its external observation of the unintended information of environmental noise to its internal observation of the intended information moving as signals through systemic channels. In the development from Shannon to Atlan, "The constructive role that surplus meaning can play was then metaphorically incorporated into the order-out-of-chaos paradigm in the recognition that noise can sometimes cause a system to reorganize at a higher level of complexity" (Hayles, 1990, p. 57). Still, as Hayles's argument moves to this climax, the informatic ventriloquizing of von Foerster's cybernetics embedded in her sources becomes acute, insofar as the "order-out-of-chaos paradigm" directly rearticulates his earlier scenario of self-organization from noise.

It may be that the ambient conceptual noise in the environment of these information-theoretic messages generated surplus meanings planting cybernetic seeds deep in my scholarly garden patch, where they lay awhile awaiting their own moment. Throughout the nineties I worked on literature, thermodynamics, and informatics. In 1997, art historian Linda Dalrymple Henderson and I co-directed the symposium "From Energy to Information." Hayles was one of the participants, and fortuitously, another participant, historian of science Timothy Lenoir, was also a coeditor of the *Writing Science* book series at Stanford University Press. Tim encouraged us to develop the symposium into an edited collection for *Writing Science*. Linda and I set to work on that project, produced a prospectus, and received an editorial suggestion that it would be good for such a volume to provide its readers with an introductory primer glossing the volume's scientific topics. This assignment fell to my lot. To the best of my recollection now, it was in the process of putting myself to school to write the chapter "From Thermodynamics to Virtuality" that I began in a serious way to follow up on some of the explicitly cybernetic references in the works on my transitional shelf (Clarke, 2002).

Several other factors dovetailed in this period. Art historian Edward Shanken broadened my cybernetic horizons with his symposium paper leading to the chapter "Cybernetics and Art: Cultural Convergence in the 1960s," focused on the British artist Roy Ascott, with significant discussions of Norbert Wiener and H. Ross Ashby (Shanken, 2002). Additionally, the *Writing Science* series was proactively bringing into English translation or scholarly currency the work of thinkers in media theory and communication studies, in systems theory and cognitive science, including Niklas Luhmann, Friedrich Kittler, and Francisco Varela, all of whom I began to read at the end of the nineties. Additionally, with the publication of her next major critical work, *How We Became Posthuman* (Hayles, 1999), Hayles and I were now on parallel tracks that converged on the contested ground of cybernetics and systems theory.

Then in the summer of 2000, I attended David Wellbery's six-week seminar on "Observation, Form, Difference: Interdisciplinary Paradigms for Literary Study" at Cornell's School of Criticism and Theory. The syllabus consisted largely of selections from Bateson's *Steps to an Ecology of Mind*, George Spencer-Brown's *Laws of Form*, and Luhmann's major work *Social Systems*. Opening Luhmann's text, one could not help but notice how consistently he referenced von Foerster's work. One can read Luhmann's text strictly as a sociological intervention, but why so constrict one's disciplinary vista? By then I was prepared to read Luhmann's systems theory as a brilliant extension of second-order cybernetics. Gathering up the von Foerster references while concurrently immersed in Luhmann's text, I proceeded to construct his particular brand of epistemological constructivism directly along the second-order line, from von Foerster's observing systems, to his protégées Maturana and Varela's concept of biological autopoiesis, to Luhmann's autopoietic "paradigm change" to a second-order theory of psychic and social systems (Luhmann, 1995, pp. 1–11). Given the conceptual weight that Luhmann's mature theory grants Spencer-Brown's calculus of distinctions in *Laws of Form*, von Foerster's famous and forceful *Whole Earth Catalog* review of it sealed the deal (von Foerster, 1970).

Also around this time, in a pure piece of "cybernetic serendipity," Linda Henderson brought an item of correspondence to my notice. Fifteen years earlier she had filed away a fan letter from a reader of *The Fourth Dimension and Non-Euclidean Geometry in Modern Art* (Henderson, 1983). The author of the letter had been unknown to her at the time, but she remembered its existence and shared it because I happened to be mentioning his name during some of our conversations. The enthusiast in question was, of course, Heinz von Foerster, whose letter also included a mimeographed map along with his open invitation for her to visit him at his home in Pescadero, California. As it turned out, the next summer it was not Linda but I who answered Heinz's invitation and followed that map to One Eden West.

My reader may have gathered by now that for me the love of cybernetics has a lot to do with the love of Heinz. I had already conceived a fondness for the ludic and challenging spirit animating his inimitable scholarly papers when I screwed up the nerve to use the contact info he had sent Linda to request an audience for myself and the recording of an interview. He was kind enough to receive me on July 20, 2001, at his kitchen table, for about 90 minutes, with his nurse hovering nearby the entire time. It turned out to be less than a year before his death.

I set my mini-cassette player running and peppered Heinz with questions. As I later determined, some of his answers were canned; one can find variations on the same basic responses in other published interviews.[2] But I think I elicited fresh observations when asking him to enlarge on his relations with Luhmann, prompting him to discourse for a few minutes on autopoiesis and Maturana's stubbornly possessive attitude toward that concept. The important takeaway was that Heinz saw nothing conceptually illicit in Luhmann's appropriation of autopoiesis for social theory. I may have also ingratiated myself to my host by requesting his opinion of my impromptu attempt to expound the argument of "Objects: Tokens for (Eigen-) Behaviors" (von Foerster, 1975). Heinz noted: "It was Varela who said, this is my most important paper" (see Clarke, 2009b, p. 30). Thinking back on it now, my main regret is that I did not draw him out on Varela more. But it would be some years still before I fully appreciated Varela's individual genius and understood how important Heinz's sponsorship had been for his arrival and reception among the systems intelligentsia at that mid-seventies moment.

I was now fully launched as a researcher into "second-order systems theory," a phrasing I coined to name the specific line of development from von Foerster, by way of Maturana and Varela, to Luhmann. Digging into Heinz's oeuvre in deeper detail, I trekked to Springer Verlag's New York outlet to take immediate possession of a copy of the new selected edition of his papers, *Understanding Understanding* (von Foerster, 2003). In 2004 I organized two panels on "Neocybernetic Emergence" for the Paris meeting of the Society for Literature and Science, from which event I would co-edit the collection *Emergence and Embodiment: New Essays on Second-Order Systems Theory* (Clarke & Hansen, 2009). In 2005 I made my first visit to the von Foerster archive at the University of Vienna's Institut für Zeitgeschichte and made the acquaintance of the invaluable Albert Müller. That same year Georg Moeller invited me to the Department of Philosophy at Brock University in St. Catharine's, Ontario, to give a talk on "Niklas Luhmann and Heinz von Foerster: The Cybernetics of Social Systems Theory," which would later be published in *Cybernetics and Human Knowing* (Clarke, 2011a). My fourth single-authored book was my first fully informed by second-order systems theory, *Posthuman Metamorphosis: Narrative and Systems* (Clarke, 2007).

I will conclude this memoir with a sketch of two separate but seminal events that combined to give my cybernetic itinerary some new twists, the repercussions of which are still playing out. The first concerns my allusion above to the systems counterculture and "Stewart Brand's Sausalito." This was the location from which Brand edited the first run of the *Whole Earth Catalog* (*WEC*) from 1968–71, and a few years later, *CoEvolution Quarterly* (*CQ*), which ran from 1974–84. Lying around my home library was a musty copy of the *Last WEC*, and occasionally I would marvel at its remarkable content. In this 400-page behemoth, Heinz's 1970 review of *Laws of Form* reappeared on page 14 in an elaborate opening section devoted to "Understanding Whole Systems." Having gained some background in cybernetics, my fascination with the *WEC* jumped to a higher level, for I could now appreciate how thoroughly cyberneticized this production was. In 2006, I presented a paper at the symposium on "The Whole Earth, Parts Thereof," at UC/Davis. This was the maiden installment of my ongoing research project "Systems Countercultures."[3]

The second major development of 2006 was my spending two sabbatical weeks that fall at the University of Massachusetts, Amherst, in the Environmental Evolution lab of the evolutionary theorist Lynn Margulis. Around 2000, browsing the science shelves at Barnes & Noble for an accessible introduction to biology to teach in my undergraduate literature and science class, I found the paperback edition of *What is Life?* (Margulis & Sagan, 2000). It was with great interest that I noted, running through their rigorous popularization of her signature theory of symbiosis as a major evolutionary dynamic, an explicit autopoietic vocabulary. It became evident that Margulis was channeling Maturana and Varela. What they stipulated as *cognition*, Margulis and Sagan called *sentience*. The common thread in both was crediting autopoiesis as the systemic form of both life and mind: "Mind and body, perceiving and living, are equally self-referring, self-reflexive processes already present in the earliest bacteria. Mind, as well as body, stems from autopoiesis. … Changing to stay the same is the essence of autopoiesis. It applies to the biosphere as well as the cell. Applied to species, it leads to evolution" (Margulis & Sagan, 2000, p. 31). Later in the same volume, one reads: "The global autopoietic system, Gaia, spins off creatures increasingly strange" (p. 190).

Elsewhere I have narrated my conversion from Gaia skeptic to Gaian thinker (Clarke, 2012a). The crux of that story is the simple, definitive datum that the Gaia hypothesis originated as a cybernetic thought experiment. As James Lovelock explained in 1972, he conceived the entity he had christened "Gaia" as "a biological cybernetic system able to homeostat the planet for an optimum physical and chemical state appropriate to its current biosphere" (p. 579). In 1975, Margulis landed *CQ* as an outlet for an early coauthored Gaia paper (Margulis & Lovelock, 1975). These two strands of my neocybernetic research program now twined together, like so: the systems counterculture as represented by *CQ* became a major venue for the Gaia hypothesis, which in due time Margulis would theorize through the concept of autopoiesis, as a direct result of meeting Maturana, Varela, von Foerster, and Atlan in 1981 at a symposium curated by Lindisfarne Association director William Irwin Thompson, who had first learned of all their work by reading *CQ* in the 1970s.

This ecologically mindful periodical, explicitly inspired by Gregory Bateson and cannily edited by Stewart Brand, still retained the format he initiated in the *WEC* of starting each further iteration with a section devoted to "Understanding Whole Systems."[4] For my current book project, "Partial Earth: Systems Theory and the Evolution of Gaia Discourse," I have been studying the nexus of intellectual activity around the *Whole Earth Catalog* and *CoEvolution Quarterly* in order to ground the cultural profundity of Gaia theory in the history of its cybernetic contexts.

NOTES

1. See Atlan (1972, pp. 232–233, 243–253). On p. 244, Atlan reproduces a diagram of self-organizing demons drawn from von Foerster (1960); see also Clarke (2014b, pp. 69–70).
2. I am not referring here to the ultimate von Foerster interview, now available in English (von Foerster, 2014).
3. Later installments include Clarke (2011b, 2012b, 2014a, and 2017).
4. See Thompson (1987). I have treated various facets of the matters compressed in this paragraph in Clarke (2009c, 2017).

REFERENCES

Atlan, H. (1972). *L'Organisation biologique et la theorie de l'information*. Paris, France: Hermann.

Bateson, G. (1972). *Steps to an ecology of mind*. New York, NY: Ballantine.

Bergthaller, H., & Schinko, C. (Eds.). (2011). *Addressing modernity: Social systems theory and U.S. cultures*. Amsterdam, the Netherlands: Rodopi.

Clarke, B. (2002). From thermodynamics to virtuality. In Clarke & Henderson (Eds.), *From energy to information* (Vol. 2002, pp. 17–33). Stanford, UK: Stanford University Press.

Clarke, B. (2007). *Posthuman metamorphosis: Narrative and systems*. New York, NY: Fordham University Press.

Clarke, B. (2009a). Heinz von Foerster's demons: The emergence of second-order systems theory. In Clarke & Hansen (Eds.), *Emergence and embodiment* (Vol. 2009, pp. 34–61). Durham, NC: Duke University Press.

Clarke, B. (2009b). Interview with Heinz von Foerster. In Clarke and Hansen (Eds.), *Emergence and embodiment* (Vol. 2009, pp. 26–33).

Clarke, B. (2009c). Neocybernetics of Gaia: The emergence of second-order Gaia theory. In E. Crist & Rinker (Eds.), *Gaia in Turmoil* (Vol. 2009, pp. 293–314). Chicago, IL: University of Chicago Press.

Clarke, B. (2011a). Heinz von Foerster and Niklas Luhmann: The cybernetics of social systems theory. *Cybernetics and Human Knowing*, *18*(3–4), 95–99.

Clarke, B. (2011b). Steps to an ecology of systems: Whole earth and systemic holism. In Bergthaller & Schinko (Eds.), Addressing modernity: Social systems theory and U.S. cultures, (Vol. 2011, pp. 259–288). Amsterdam, the Netherlands: Rodopi.

Clarke, B. (2012a). "'Gaia is not an organism': The early scientific collaboration of Lynn Margulis and James Lovelock. In Sagan (Ed.), *Lynn Margulis: The life and legacy of a scientific rebel* (Vol. 2012, pp. 32–43). White River Junction, VT: Chelsea Green.

Clarke, B. (2012b). From information to cognition: The systems counterculture, Heinz von Foerster's pedagogy, and second-order cybernetics. *Constructivist Foundations, 7*(3), 196–207.

Clarke, B. (2014a). John Lilly. *The Mind of the Dolphin, and Communication out of Bounds. Communication* +, *1*(8), 3. <http://scholarworks.umass.edu/cpo/vol3/iss1/8>.

Clarke, B. (2014b). *Neocybernetics and narrative*. Minneapolis, MN: University of Minnesota Press.

Clarke, B. (2017). Planetary immunity: Biopolitics, Gaia theory, the holobiont, and the systems counterculture. In Hörl (Ed.), with Burton 2017 *On general ecology: The new ecological paradigm* (pp. 193–215). London, UK: Bloomsbury.

Clarke, B., & Hansen, M. B. N. (Eds.). (2009). *Emergence and embodiment: New essays in second-order systems theory*. Durham, NC: Duke University Press.

Clarke, B., & Henderson, L. D. (Eds.). (2002). *From energy to information: Representation in science and technology, art, and literature*. Stanford, UK: Stanford University Press.

Crist, E., & Rinker, H. B. (Eds.). (2009). *Gaia in turmoil: Climate change, biodepletion, and earth ethics in an age of crisis*. Cambridge, MA: MIT Press.

Gleick, J. (1987). *Chaos: Making a new science*. New York, NY: Penguin Books.

Hayles, N. K. (1990). *Chaos bound: Orderly disorder in contemporary literature and science*. Ithaca, NY: Cornell University Press.

Hayles, N. K. (1999). *How we became Posthuman: Virtual bodies in cybernetics, literature, and informatics*. Chicago, IL: University of Chicago Press.

Henderson, L. D. (1983). *The fourth dimension and non-euclidean geometry in modern art*. Princeton, NJ: Princeton University Press.

Hörl, E. (Ed.), with Burton, (2017) J. *On general ecology: The new ecological paradigm*. London, UK: Bloomsbury.

Lem, S. (1985). *The cyberiad: Fables for the cybernetic age*. Trans. Michael Kandel. New York, NY: Harvest.

Lovelock, J. (1972). Gaia as seen through the atmosphere. *Atmospheric Environment, 6*(8), 579–580. doi:10.1016/0004-6981(72)90076-5

Luhmann, N. (1995). *Social systems, trans. J. Bednarz, Jr. with D. Baecker*. Stanford, UK: Stanford University.

Margulis, L., & Lovelock, J. (1975). The atmosphere as circulatory system of the biosphere: The Gaia hypothesis. *CoEvolution Quarterly (Summer), 5*, 31–40.

Margulis, L., & Sagan, D. (2000). *What is life?* Berkeley, CA: University of California Press.

Paulson, W. R. (1988). *The noise of culture: Literary texts in a world of information*. Ithaca, NY: Cornell University Press.

Sagan, D. (Ed.). (2012). *Lynn Margulis: The life and legacy of a scientific rebel*. White River Junction, VT: Chelsea Green.

Serres, M. (1982). *Hermes: Literature, science, philosophy*. J. V. Harari & D. F. Bell (Eds.). Baltimore, MA: Johns Hopkins University Press.

Shanken, E. (2002). Cybernetics and art: Cultural convergence in the 1960s. In Clarke & Henderson (Eds.), *From energy to information: Representation in science and technology, art, and literature* (Vol. 2002, pp. 255–277). Stanford, UK: Stanford University Press.

Shannon, C., & Weaver, W. (1949). *The mathematical theory of communication*. Urbana, IL: University of Illinois Press.

Thompson, W. I. (Ed.). (1987). *Gaia—A way of knowing: Political implications of the new biology*. Great Barrington, MA: Lindisfarne Press.

von Foerster, H. (1960). On self-organizing systems and their environments. *In Von Foerster, 2003*, pp. 1–19.

von Foerster, H. (1970). Laws of form. Whole Earth Catalog (Spring), 12.

von Foerster, H. (1975). Objects: Tokens for (Eigen-)behaviors. *In Von Foerster*, 2003, pp. 261–271.

von Foerster, H. (2003). *Understanding understanding: Essays on cybernetics and cognition*. New York, NY: Springer.

von Foerster, H. (2014). *The beginning of heaven and Earth has no name: Seven days with second-order cybernetics*, A. Müller & K. H. Müller (Eds.), trans. E. Rooks and M. Kasenbacher. New York, NY: Fordham University Press.

von Foerster, H., & Poerksen, B. (2002). *Understanding systems: Conversations on epistemology and ethics*. New York, NY: Kluwer Academic/Plenum Publishers.

THE LEAGUE

Frank Galuszka

About painting, cybernetics, and shared purpose, this article is partly a story, in part a memoir, an adventure in cybernetics, happening 30 years ago, in snow, in the small Swiss city of St. Gallen. A conference of the American Society for Cybernetics meets there. It is 1987. The author, a painter, searching for a new understanding of painting, encounters a convergence of the art of painting and the art of cybernetics through principles of second-order cybernetics in Pask, von Foerster and Maturana, dissolved in Kathleen Forsythe's poetry. The form, as well as the content of this article, reflects cybernetics.

Painting, symbol as well as unbeatable medium of individual consciousness, thrives when people are interested in, and revere, the reality of their own and other people's minds and hearts. Painting can't make anyone interested and reverent. It can only reward interest and reverence that are brought to it, in a social milieu of respectful persons.

—Peter Schjeldahl (1990, p. 97)

Ludwig Richter relates in his reminiscences how once, when he was in Tivoli as a young man, he and three friends set out to paint part of the landscape, all four firmly resolved not to deviate from nature by a hair's breadth; and although the subject was the same, and each quite creditably reproduced what his eyes had seen, the result was four totally different pictures, as different from each other as the personalities of the four painters. Whence the narrator drew the conclusion that there is no such thing as objective vision, and that form and color are always apprehended differently according to temperament.

—Heinrich Wolfflin (1915, p. 1)

The fact that I myself, at the moment of painting, do not understand my own pictures, does not mean that these pictures have no meaning; on the contrary, their meaning is so profound, complex, coherent and involuntary that it escapes the most simple analysis of logical intuition.

—Salvador Dali (1935, p. 559)

1.

Paintings are still and silent. They are materially obvious things. Yet paintings seem curiously apart from themselves, as if referencing unseen elsewheres.

There is a dislocation; sometimes a lack of traction. As if there is nothing to be seen except irrelevant rhetoric. Paintings invite time. What is absent in them can have the feeling of simple apartness, or remoteness, or even a sense of being intentionally hidden. What is absent, we can speculate, is an obscure message of some kind. We can imagine that this message is intentionally hidden, as it might be in a religious painting that seems to disclose and obscure its mystery simultaneously. Or we can feel that the consciousness, which attended the creation of the painting, has erased its presence and moved on. Or that this consciousness is too fundamentally unlike our own to be understood, or too distant because of a cultural or temporal remoteness, or a feeling of exclusion from a contemporary *avant garde* milieu that might have produced this work. Maybe it is just us. We do not know enough, or feel enough, or care enough to get into the painting.

Some paintings coincide with themselves more than others. When we feel the consciousness of the painter integrated with the painting before us, as perhaps in the case of, say, the familiar style of Rembrandt or Cezanne, we feel a certain relief, a coziness, a coming home to something that accepts us. Because of the fame of the artist we are also assured that we have stepped in front of something worth looking at. Still, there are things that are distant, inaccessible, and obdurate. The maddening simplicity of a surface covered by paint.

The painting may seem a wall between visions. The viewer may feel rebuffed.

Some of this is due to the confusion over the role, or even the existence, of "talent." Of creativity as a door, both open and closed to understanding. There is suspicion of swindle. "Is this really as good as they say?" Alienation from the artwork is maybe due to the mystery of mastery, or of cryptic underlying compositional gambits, or to an opaque and politically suspect establishment of authorities and interpreters of art. Some comes from a lack of traction with the dense nonverbal thinking that produced the work.

We are looking at a reality that seems alien to us. It is our constructions of reality that disagree. This is not only true for representational painting. All paintings organize value, importance, meaningfulness. At the sight of a confident but disagreeing reality, we become self-conscious of our own. The temptation to dismiss the reality of the other is strong.

While art history and art theory produce much valuable information about the cultural significance of an artwork, they tell us little about how it was done. And even they tell us only a small part of the story about why it was done.

It is curious that art history and art theory, for the most part, have developed alongside the creation of artworks, in this case paintings, and have more to say about the perspectives of viewers of art rather than creators of art. While their findings and commentaries have much value to art and its understanding, in the end they do not penetrate into revealing much about its creation.

2.

I was introduced to cybernetics because Bob Schoenholtz lived on the same street I lived on. His daughter and my daughter were friends. Bob was interested in advanced ideas about psychology. He had been an employee of my father-in-law. This is how it is in Philadelphia. Everybody knows everybody. It is like a village.

Bob introduced me to Harvey Horowitz. Bob was a psychologist; Harvey a psychiatrist. Both of them were crazy about Gregory Bateson.

They said to me, as if the word itself would persuade or hypnotize me: "Circularity." I thought, in response, "Big deal."

But I was, from even before this time, on a collision course with cybernetics.

I was a painter. I not only wanted to be a painter, I wanted to be a great painter. In those days it was acceptable and even admirable to want to do great things.

I studied how it was I might become a great painter. I studied composition and style. I studied art history and art criticism. I painted like an old master and like an avant gardist. I did realism and conceptual art.

Nothing I studied got me where I wanted to go. Everything described quite a bit about art, but even the most erudite criticism seemed to be missing the point.

I read biographies of great artists and painted hundreds of paintings. I talked with artists about art endlessly.

All of these concerns seemed to be existing within something that was much larger.

Bob said Circularity. Harvey said Circularity.

3.

Contemporary life, even then, was fast. Painting is slow. Success in painting is advanced through dedication and patience. Painting requires introspection. Introspection is distinct from narcissism. It is best to have an uncluttered mind, to be free of distractions. Multi-tasking is the enemy of painting. Painting is an activity and a non-activity. Painting is partly conscious and partly unconscious. Because painting is partly unconscious, the painter is painting 24 hours a day. Even when the painter is not physically painting, or not thinking about painting, the painter is painting. This is why long walks alone, silence, and sleeping are all valuable parts of painting.

I write as a painter. My view is that painting is a constructivist practice. I believe that all painting is constructivist, regardless of style or -ism, and regardless of the intention of the painter. By saying that painting is a constructivist practice I mean that the painter has recourse to no other criteria, except in a trivial sense, than that which comes about in the process of painting, which is circular and closed.

It is in acceptance of painting as a closed system that painting mysteriously opens.

The painter is aware that the painting is a result of internal operations of the painter, or has the impression that the painting creates itself, using the painter as a medium. The painter is in communication with physical and intellectual factors, the paint itself, himself, an imagined other or others, the times we are in, the history of the painting, its visual pathways and its evidence of accumulated decisions, the subject of the painting, the planning of it, and so on.

These factors, even down to the original subject (or concept) itself, the motivation or pretext for the painting's existence, may be subject to change as the painting develops. The painter usually resists this change in the beginning. But it is not unusual to feel the original pretext disappear in the course of the work, and often as the last major decision that allows the work to "find itself," to resolve into the emergent structure of its own integrity. This integrity often appears with a breakdown of the artist's control over the artwork, and severs the artist's identification with the artwork, giving the impression that the painting has become, through this seemingly necessary sacrificial act, independent of its creator. This arrival at independence has not usually been a conscious purpose or destination from the point of view of the painter, and it is with mixed feelings that the painting concludes, and is "finished."

Some artists seek to cling to some things, the audience, the subject, the plan, and so on, while others tolerate or entertain universal and mutual flexibility. These highly flexible artists are the most interesting to me, as their process most vividly resembles Maturana's diagram of structural coupling and drift.

4.

Bob said Circularity. Harvey said Circularity.

I had dinner with them and had nice meals on pewter plates at Bob's house. They talked about Gregory Bateson and gave me two books to read. You know which books they are.

I liked the metalogues best.

What is an instinct? An instinct is an explanatory principle.

Sometime later Heinz came to Philadelphia to speak. I met him at Harvey's house. Heinz had taken the train from New York through the industrial ruins of North Philadelphia. "It is a museum of decay!" he declared. I knew what he was talking about. I had been painting the same things. Those buildings. That decay. I commuted on the same rails. I saw the same ruins. Every day. Over and over. Buildings, rubble, graffiti, under the brooding rain-heavy North Philadelphia skies.

After his speech on the usual things he spoke about, circling around that we do not see that we do not see, I went home and lay awake sleepless. I did not sleep for eight days. No sleep. No sleep at all.

5.

On the blackboard at the University of St. Gallen, on a snowy afternoon, Humberto Maturana drew an eye with his chalk up in one corner.

His hair was more or less still black. A little gray, a gray scarf, a peasant shepherd's hat. There is one chalk-drawn circle next to another, side by side, each with an arrow showing it is meant to be a cycle, and with a flat line beneath.

In the course of his lecture the two circles become deformed as does the flat line underneath. Everything adjusts to everything else. The living systems. The living systems in relationship, the line beneath, now alive and springing with a serpentine curve, indicating the medium. Then there is the eye in the corner of the chalkboard. He says there must always be an eye.

In these days, with the snow outside and the cement walls of the buildings damp in the spots where the snow wants most to melt, and the wooden walkway up from the town dusted with snow, Maturana's presentation, and his use of certain words, like "multiversa," are controversial. There are factions and marvelous arguments against him; there is a crackling in the air. It seemed he is just on the threshold of winning the day. Everything about the conference feels like massing energy on the crest of a wave. I am new to cybernetics, to these conversations and arguments, to these people. I have tumbled as if from nowhere, with my past utterly negated, into this energy on the crest of this wave. At first I feel that I am accidentally here. Unable to speak. In this transparent and unknown world. There is the excruciating conspicuous loneliness of the yet-to-be-initiated—the conspicuous lack of anyone to talk with at the first of the social gatherings, at a lively reception where everyone else that comes in from the cold has someone they are excited to see again and nobody cares about you. Wondering why you came. All that. Going to dinner alone. In a strange town. Eating one dessert after another. Then a strange character dashes through the dim light of the restaurant under the low vaults, a character with a cape and a toy weapon of a walking stick—pursued by admirers, who stack themselves at a table in the brown night, ordering obscurely from a waiter who makes change out of a large black leather pocket book.

At the table it is Gordon Pask and his retinue. I am invited in from my isolation and my second *creme caramel* into that. With nothing to say, but suddenly in a somewhere.

6.

A painting is an object among objects. Yet it suggests that it is not an object. It can be created so as to enhance or reduce its paintedness, shifting its weight from one identity to another. The judgment of the artist about this decision is always of interest. Slick illusionism strikes viewers as miraculous but withholding. Obvious paintedness, or painterliness, seems perhaps humbler and more accessible. It seems to make less of a transcendental claim. Perhaps the failure of the object to coincide with itself is mitigated by painterliness, or "healed" by it, as the painting is inducted more explicitly into the material world.

7.

At the table people are not saying impossibly intellectual things, but doing what people always do, gossiping, catching up, jockeying for favor. A little candle. The faces in the light. Animated. A single light in an amber bowl in the middle of the table, and our shadows curving above us, crawling across the low intersecting vaulting.

8.

There is a book by Herman Hesse called *Journey to the East* (1932). I know you know it. And in this book there is a questing club, the League, and they quest in Switzerland or Swabia. For something obscure. They find and they do not find. They argue and the little society falls to pieces.

This is where I was before it fell to pieces. At this table I am in this book. I am in the *Journey to the East*.

The fact that I myself, at the moment of understanding, do not understand my own understandings, does not mean that these understandings have no meaning.

9.

It is distinctions in personal style that Wofflein notes in the retelling of Ludwig Richter's story of artists in the field, devoted to faithfully rendering nature, and coming up with very different results. These artists each had an individual sensibility that, in playing with or against prevailing cultural style, resulted in distinct individual styles. The constructivist underpinnings of style are revealed in this variation among practitioners linked by motif, technique, culture, esthetic environment, and education.

Artists who paint the world from life, such as *plein air* painters, intensely observe, but rarely observe themselves observing, no matter how focused they are. An interesting exception is Cezanne, who paints the external subject and his awareness of himself painting it at the same time. Look at his paintings that way. I think you will see what I mean.

10.

It seems that every cybernetics conference begins with complaining and ends with happiness. That in the beginning of every conference everyone says "this conference isn't very good" or "it isn't as good as the last one." That in the course of the conference something happens to consciousness, and community arises.

Even after three days of conferencing there are sad farewells. And difficulty reentering civilian life.

The secret is that these conferences are the journey to the East. That something is discovered in each, and forgotten afterward. That in the soul of every conference is anamnesis.

It is like this in painting. After every painting you forget how to paint.

Toward the end of every painting there is an awakening, "Oh! This is how to paint!" And afterward, forgetting how to paint.

The deepest secret of these cybernetics conferences is this: That when, in conversation, two people agree that human communication is impossible (and demonstrate convincingly why this is) and convince each other of the fact, then human communication suddenly becomes possible.

When, after a long struggle, a painting feels it is a failure, success mysteriously dawns.

11.

I made a presentation the next day. I talked about something. I remember showing a slide of a woman in a blue room taking something out of a drawer or putting it in. Who cares what it was.

The snow fell every day.

I found my little society. I fell in with new friends.

Looking over the ancient library in St. Gallen you have to wear cloth shoes over your shoes. Like sacks for your feet. Blue.

As we are shuffling across the rooms with their archaic bent windows and walls, Maturana appears at a threshold with the pristine white light of the snow outside reflecting up through the windows from below to illuminate the curved plaster ceilings, recognizing us from the conference, declaring, "We are in the brotherhood of the shoes!" The blue shoes. The blue shoes that tied up behind our feet.

12.

Out of an invisible sensibility visible style is created.

Artists unite theory and practice. They operate out of a sensibility rather than by mechanically applying theory to practice.

13.

It can be that all conferences on all topics affect the consciousness of participants in such a way. That for this reason or that reason they are all magic-making incantations. It can be that all conferences on all topics produce (unforeseen) enchanted harmonies. But no others can discuss this coherently in the happening of it. Cybernetics is a mechanics of something. What is it a mechanics of?

In St. Gallen I was in the place of finding after so much looking. In the Cathedral of St. Gallen I encountered (above a confessional) a carved and gilded representation of the parable of the lost drachma, with a woman and a broom, searching, while all around her there are windows open to the light. Everything spills into everything. Everything incandesces with the dimensionalizing light of converging illuminations.

Coming out of the cathedral and knowing that discovery-invention is now fully and exclusively present I ask Penny Colville as we are walking down the stairs with Kathleen Forsythe and her friend Dik behind us talking about something else, in the snow, about Conversation Theory. As an insider with Pask I know she will know, and she does, describing-enacting how Gordon himself once described it at a social event, picking up three oranges that happen to be near and juggling them. While the meaning is admittedly now unclear to me in retrospect, it is its perfect coherence in the moment that I remember, and the fact that I actually saw Penny juggling these invisible-but-visible oranges as simultaneous snowballs as we walked down the stairs.

14.

There was a workshop in Horsham, Pennsylvania, and a closed circuit video of a family in group therapy, and one of the members of the family was full of members himself. He had what they then called multiple personality disorder. I taught at a school with my students from the so-called inner city. They said, I act one way when I am here, I act another way when I am home—which is the real me?

Each of these personalities is exclusively present when they are present. The other personality was nowhere to be seen.

The person at the clinic in Horsham said he had 112 personalities. He was not unhappy about it.

Heinz von Foerster said, "I am not one man. I am a whole collection of people."

> *... although the subject was the same, and each quite creditably reproduced what his eyes had seen, the result was four totally different pictures ... .*

I wondered if I could create a second-order style of painting out of this circumstance.

15.

In the airport in Zurich, after the astute metal detectors had located the fillings in my teeth, Kathleen, again clothed in violet and lavender, who was going out on one flight as I was going on another, and we were passing in the terminal, handed me a pile of pink xeroxed pages clipped together. It was a book. It was a book of poems. It was called *Warrior of the Gentle Passion*.

I began reading it while they were deicing the plane. I read the last page as we touched down at JFK.

What characterized the art world, as well of the rest of sophisticated culture that I had been living in, was a distancing attitude of irony which was absent in Kathleen's book of poems.

This book might have been opaque to me a week earlier. But now it was transparent. I saw into it.

Not only was defensive irony absent from Kathleen's book of poems, but it had been absent from the conference. It was absent from the Journey to the East.

We had stepped over despair. The forthright loving agenda of Kathleen Forsythe's poems was the kind of thing that was commonly dismissed (with ridicule) in the world I knew, in which heartfelt emotion was lumped together with kitsch and cheap sentimentality. And in which emotion, love specifically, had been as doctrinally alienated from thinking as church was separated from state. But cybernetics was in the business, in Forsythe's work, of making the world whole. Her work required something of the reader. It required the kind

Frank Galuszka, "Inga" 2012 65 × 85" acrylic on canvas, used with permission.

of undefended courage she wrote about, a courage that included exchanging the dead-end comforts of social acceptance in shared despair, distraction and vanity, for the will to construct in mind and action something beyond it, an optimism and a future waiting to be invented from the possible and neglected worlds-that-might-be-built that were close at hand, in which, like painting, cybernetics thrives among people who are interested in, and revere, the reality of their own and other people's minds and hearts.

REFERENCES

Dali, S. (1935). *The conquest of the irrational.* (David Gascogne, Trans.). New York: Julian Levy Gallery. (Reprinted in Dali, p. 559, 2004, Philadelphia Museum of Art, catalog).

Hesse, H. (1932). *The journey to the east* (Hilda Rosner, Trans.). (2003) London, UK: Picador (Macmillan).

Schjeldahl, P. (1990). *The new low.* Village Voice (New York), 13 November 1990: 97. (Re-printed in: Columns and catalogues, by P. Schjeldahl, 1994. Great Barrington, MA: The Figures.)

Wolfflin, H. (1915). *Principles of art history, the problem of the development of style in later art.* (M. D. Hottinger, Trans. (1932)). Mineola, NY: Dover Publications.

WINKY DINK AND ME: ORIGINS

Paul Pangaro

Through early childhood experiences and then recollections of the many cyberneticians he knew in the 1970s and 1980s, the author traces his personal trajectory toward interaction design and cybernetics. He moves from fascination with technology, through disillusionment about Artificial Intelligence, to seeing that living in cybernetics is a journey of return to uncertainty, risk, and possibility.

'The joy of creating ideas, new and eternal, in and of a world, old and temporal, robots have it not. For this my Mother bore me.'

—Warren S. McCulloch, 1970, p. 87.

SCREEN

Figure 1. Winky Dink.

My first interactive technology pleasure is named "Winky Dink." The theme song goes, "Winky Dink (pause) and me, Winky Dink (pause) and you ... ." Winky Dink's TV show is called *Winky Dink and You.* I am 4 years old, and the "you" is me.

I focus intently on the small, glowing TV screen just inches from my eyes. Winky Dink has a round face and a big, star-shaped hairdo (Mentzer, 2013) (Figure 1). Winky Dink is my friend. His TV show is full of gray monochrome adventure. Its animation is rendered by cross-fades between static hand drawings. Winky Dink dances and moves in his stop-action way, all the while setting the stage for my part to come. I pull out my interface tools: A plastic, aquamarine-colored sheet to cover the screen, held taut by static electricity from the screen's magnetic field; crayons for drawing on the screen. My interface is enabled. The first frame appears with a few seemingly random lines on it. Winky Dink smiles reassuringly in a corner. I trace the lines and make fat, gloppy streaks on my display. I bathe in electromagnetic waves. Another frame appears, with different lines, Winky Dink in a different corner, still smiling. I trace these lines, also, participant in the scene, interacting with self-importance. A third and then fourth frame and then suddenly letters appear from my tracings to form words, and the words are a message about the next show. Now I know what will happen with Winky Dink tomorrow! I see into Winky Dink's future!

And for me, what of my future? Even then I felt destined to be a member of the programmed digerati. For decades to come I sit before keyboards and screens and graphical interfaces claiming to be "user-friendly"—*but as friendly as Winky Dink?* I will connect to vast networks of communities via mobile devices with facial-recognition security—*but will I be OK?* In my earliest childhood memories, human interactions are unpredictable, threatening, and perilous, while technology seems predicable, friendly, and safe. With Winky Dink, *I feel better because I can control the world through my interactions.*

VOICE

My childhood is rich with singing and piano-playing, by parents, aunts and uncles, brothers, and cousins. Opera is constantly heard, poetry often read, performances of plays often seen and sometimes performed by me (angel in a Christmas pageant; prophetess in a cub-scout show).

Into a wall socket I insert the plug coming from a child-sized suitcase, its canvas surfaces of plaid design. I flip the power lever, place the arm over a fresh, new 45-RPM vinyl record, and listen to the voice of Domenico Modugno. "*Volare!*," he sings in Italian, *to fly! Contare!*, I sing with him, *to sing!* For the next 2 hours I do nothing else but sing the same song, over and over. I learn it all, every rise of the voice, every lilt of joy to have his fantasy:

Penso che un sogno cosi' non ritorni mai piu'

[I do not think a dream like this one can ever come back]

With his screen, Winky Dink guides my hand. When I interact with him I get a message that is more about him than about me. With his voice, Domenico Modugno makes a suggestion, offers an example. By starting from his place, *I see where I might go.* My history is the threading of those two themes: technology that shows itself as friendly yet constrains; and relationships that demand much more but "let fly." I am to learn that this is the difference between computer science and cybernetics and between the computers of today and the possibilities of tomorrow.

USER CONTROL

Wikipedia claims Winky Dink is "the first interactive electronic medium" and "interactive TV" (Winky & You, n.d.). But of course, no matter what I do, Winky Dink just keeps going. He pretends to respond to me, *making me think I matter*. This is simply a precursor to our life with digital technology today, where Facebook, Snapchat, Google, and other massive Internet platforms fulfill their business models at human expense (Harris, 2016).

Today's digital technologies tend to glorify the meaning of "interactive" through "services" that are more responsive than Winky Dink. But they serve their own needs more than mine or yours or anyone else's. Technologies control the dialog and do not much notice if I am not there. Still, when Winky Dink smiles or when online "friends" say they "like" me, I feel better. Winky Dink, genderless and beguiling, guides me from a glowing screen, bright and warm with promise of participation. But each screen is just a way to narrow human action to programmed response. First I am programmed to buy devices and then I am programmed to tap and scribble on their screens (Solon, 2017). I put commitment into my actions but mistake my actions as originating with me. Today's digital technologies are mostly like that too, because us "users" do far more of what they want than what we want. (The term "user" was invented so we could all feel better about what we were using.)

MARVIN AND SEYMOUR

Through grammar school and high school, the attractive glow of screens burns bright in my imagination. Technology more advanced than TV is only available to me in the books on the engineering shelves of my local library. I read every one. I enter the Massachusetts Institute of Technology (MIT) as an undergrad in 1969 and discover a place swirling with bright people and bright ideas and chunky technology in every corner. Never having seen a computer before, now I sit at huge, powerful machines, with screens that offer far more than my old TV ever did. Computers give me confidence that *I* can determine what it will do, because I myself write lines of instructions whose details *it* must follow. *I mistake this reliability for a relationship, but it makes me feel better.*

MIT swirls with Marvin Minsky and Seymour Papert talking artificial intelligence (AI). They are talking symbolic programming, not the subset of AI that has overwhelmed the world since 2016, called "machine learning" (which they tried hard to kill; Pangaro, 2017)). At MIT they are the high priests of AI. They lecture in tag-team format: One steps up to knock out an idea until it's on the ropes, then the other guy comes in to knock out the next one. Minsky writes a book called *Computation: Finite and Infinite Machines*. Its title is dramatic. Its diagrams are clean and perfectly clear, and its concepts are elegant. It reduces computation to its sterilized essence: "Turing machines," the conceptual breakthrough that was the blueprint for making digital machines (Minsky, 1967).

My first personal Turing Machine is a PDP-7 computer, 8 K of magnetic core memory, no disk storage at all. But it has something very rare for that time; a screen that I could program, simple line drawings, slow animations, aquamarine on dark gray, *my very own Winky Dink.*

I AM ADDICTED

Sitting here I forge my future. I study AI. I write code for smart programs that solve puzzles. But just like the beautiful, albeit dispassionate diagrams in Minky's book, the processes of AI are ascetic, body-less, unconvincing. Can our complex brain be doing that trivial dance of zero-and-one logic, like digital computers? Humans are a mess with emotions and irrationality, and these programs of data-driven binary steps are rigid, formulaic, un-compelling. I am uncomfortable with human interactions—*are they not unreliable?* Studying humanities brings such pleasure (MIT's expert courses in Shakespeare, Chaucer, playwriting, acting). These are some of my guides to rejecting AI. Like the name says, AI is artificial and just does not fit my experience of being human. *I live in the contradictions of wanting to interact with machines I can explain and control; of wanting human interactions that are more reliable and fulfilling. Of ultimately wanting to make machines more human.* I am no longer satisfied with computers or with Winky Dink or with AI. Disillusioned, I go drifting. Until I meet Jerry.

JERRY

Artificial intelligence and its instrumentality, digital computers, were of the church of MIT, but there were less promoted and more subversive enchanters lurking. Jerry Lettvin, neurophysiologist and MD without PhD, taught biology. You have to take his class, everyone said. But biology did not interest me. *I want to avoid the messiness and wetness of the body if I can, the likely cause of unreliable human interactions.* But here, in the spell of Jerry's lectures, the organism is no longer an input/output machine, like a computer; it is part of a loop from perception to action and back again to perception. It does not seek knowledge for its own sake (like science, like AI); it acts in order to know in order to act (Pickering, 2015). Jerry begins my education in cybernetics.

On the outside, Jerry's method of "teaching" is one of building arguments; but it's really a form of cognitive seduction. You can only love the ideas that come from him, because they caress your thinking. Minsky and Papert knock them around; Jerry breathes them into life.

I graduate with a BS in Humanities/Computer Science and pursue projects with Jerry in building computer models of how the axon trees of the nervous system might process the codes that travel in a train of nerve impulses. His research lab is the only one asking this question—nowhere else at MIT and nearly nowhere else—even today (Cariani, 2007 is a rare exception). Jerry sits at the aquamarine lines on the display of my personal Turing Machine, my PDP-7, controlling the inputs and watching the outputs, making the simulated nervous system dance with him. It is a *pas de deux* I never forget. (My close relationship with him brings me one of the most affectionate moments of my life: His bear hug, in front of his class in the biggest MIT lecture hall, on my birthday. *It is a warm hug and he lifts me easily off the ground, to a great height.*) From here on I find individuals like Jerry irresistible, more than any technology could be, and I pursue a path of finding them, in history or in the flesh.

WARREN AND ROOK

If Jerry never mentions cybernetics, all the time he mentions Warren McCulloch. McCulloch was a legend, a genius, a poet, a profoundly original thinker. McCulloch and Lettvin and others had been looking at the nervous system in ways that others had not: With an organic sensuality that brought the experience of living to their work. McCulloch was a deep influence on Minsky and Papert, many would say (and they themselves would say; e.g., Papert, 1965).

McCulloch's contemporary, Norbert Wiener, had coined the word "cybernetics" with his colleagues (Wiener, 1948) because they wanted to name a new discipline, one to embody what steering a ship is about: Having a goal, aiming for it, getting blown off course, adjusting and re-aiming, and so on (Pangaro, 2012). It was McCulloch who was perhaps the single most important force behind cybernetics as a movement and a discipline—yes, more than Wiener, because of his organizing of a conference series called the Macy Meetings that forever imprint the concepts of cybernetics on the culture of scientific thought (Heims, 1991).

Warren McCulloch dies in the month I arrive at MIT, September 1969. But in the mid-1980s I visit the McCulloch Farm in Old Lyme, Connecticut, a handful of times, at the invitation of Rook, Warren's widow. She was a critical force at the farm and in her husband's orbit (as was Mai von Foerster, Heinz von Foerster's wife, who I knew in a later era). After a meal that is rich with love and conversation, she sits with her guests amid myriad books and plays LPs of music that is important to her. Her stories of Warren are definitive, of course. On one occasion I visited Rook and her family with Gordon Pask, who looked up to Warren as to a father (as Gordon himself would say). Walking with Gordon across the farm, past the horse stables on a very windy night, I say it feels like Warren is still emphatically present. Gordon, with his cape flapping uncontrollably, agrees with a grave seriousness. But I am getting ahead of introducing the protagonist of my story.

GORDON

I learn the richest meaning of cybernetics from Gordon Pask. I am in my first-ever full-time job, a position on research staff at the MIT Architecture Machine

Group (Wright Steenson, 2017). In the job interview I show the head of the group, Nicholas Negroponte, the computer-animated films I made with my collaborators on the PDP-7. The job is mine. (Eight years later, Nicholas morphs ArchMach and some other MIT research groups into the MIT Media Lab.) I do not recall how long into the job but one fateful day I walk into Nicholas's office to find Pask standing at a desk, looking down at papers with his head tilted sideways and lighting his peculiar metal pipe. "Hello, Paul, how-do?," Gordon Pask says to me, his side-angle gaze reaching toward me. *His aura is both friendly sprite and probing sorcerer.* Nicholas tells Gordon I am an "actor" (having been in MIT student productions continuously for the last four of my five undergraduate years) and tells me that Gordon is a "producer and writer for the stage." I shall always be grateful for that start; it was as if Nicholas wanted to distill each of us to an essence that the other would recognize. I do not think he predicted that *I would get hooked on the performance, hooked on the man, hooked on the cybernetics.*

At Negroponte's lab Pask plays the role of genius critic and cybernetician of conversation, bearing a general theory of everything and a gender-bending pharmacopeia, all of which he is willing to share. Pask's cybernetics says everything arises from interaction ("In the beginning was the interaction" is how I paraphrase it later). And I learn so much from my interactions with him. I recognize the way I had always experienced the world, before I could articulate it—*we exist in interaction, even if unreliable and scary.* Here is someone who has made a framework for me, far beyond reliable computers and inhumane AI, richly generative and with a sensibility I can relate to. A spirit of performance and participation, *of being alive.*

We talk at length that first day and, following a pattern that would be repeated for the decade to come, we continue into dinner at a noisy restaurant where listening is a strain, and then late into the night where amazing ideas meld with dreaming. There is always more to know, more to ask, more to be fascinated by. For every idea I could speak, Gordon has so much to say. I ask how his human-made artifacts could have attributes that humans have, such as intelligence (Pask, 1980). And most of all, how could his machines hold conversations with humans or with each other (Pask, 1961, 1982). These questions occupy my waking and sleeping dreams from now onward.

On the paper placemat he sketches out his first performance/art installation, Musicolour (Pask, 1971). Having been immersed in the world of Turing machines and symbolic computing and then seduced and prepared by Jerry, my eyes are ready to see how Paskian machines, made even from crude technologies of the 1950s and 1960s, create possibilities within generative, unpredictable, novel interactions *that are conversations.* And why would I want anything else—with computers I thought I was in control, with that do-my-bidding power that all computer hackers are supposed to seek (Weizenbaum, 1976). But Gordon had another way: To see interaction as a *shared participation and responsibility.* Neither *controls* the outcomes. Each is an agent. I could reframe my history, no longer casting myself as victim of unreliability.

I could be responsible for what I bring to the relationship and for what I want from it, and negotiate. *The unreliability of human exchange becomes an opening of possibility and not a closing down.* Someday this will be my framing of interaction design.

After dinner on this same first night we head back to his hotel room with intent, where Pask performs an archeological dig through oversized leather luggage to fetch a particular journal paper. Beyond the layers of white permanent-press shirts and double-breasted suit jackets are crinkled plastic bags containing bottles of pharmaceuticals. Next, spare wire and wiring connectors and tools, all loose and strewn about. Finally a compressed "wadge" of reprints and overhead transparencies emerges with his goal within it, a small pink pamphlet with tiny, rusted staples: *An Outline Theory of Media for Education and Entertainment* (Pask, 1976). It is well after 1 a.m. and I begin to take my leave. But wait, he wants to give me his business card. Another archeological dig, this time into his jacket. Double-breasted and always a visual frame for a tie-able bow-tie (defined as a "proper bow-tie"), his jacket weighs probably eight pounds, every pocket stuffed with materials all essential to his daily living. Tobacco tins, pipe, cigarettes, lighter, matches, pills, thick wads of papers, passport, small screwdrivers used for cleaning his pipe. ... We review nearly all of these with audio identification and affirming commentary, all while he seeks his business card. *I realize every item is a prop, every comment a means to have a personal conversation, all to linger in the interaction.*

Finally, his business card appears as if from up his sleeve, stained with pipe ashes, corners crumpled. I express my thanks as best I can, as much my gratitude for his existence as for the evening together. I try to leave gracefully and walk down the hall but he keeps speaking from his hotel room door, his words trailing off to inaudibility. As I walk to the elevator, the paisley in the hotel's wallpaper dances to ideas that are swirling within me.

TRANSITION

Although previously steeped in all the hardware and software and concepts that MIT could offer, I know quickly that nothing is more interesting than Pask. And most useful of all, I could read his papers and write code. So I drop out of Negroponte's PhD program (his first-ever PhD student, for all of a matter of weeks) and flee MIT for New York and its cheap flights to London. (Nicholas understands my defection and is completely gracious about it.) To England I go and impose myself on Pask's time, his lab people, and his family. All of them were, of course, used to it: Unknown student-type appears with paisley in his eyes and wants in.

RITUALS

I ring the bell at the front door. It swings open to reveal a roundish, slightly stern woman with glasses who says, "I am Elizabeth Pask"—Gordon's wife.

She is cordial but a bit cold, weary it seems of yet another meal to be served to a new visitor of unknown quality. "Gordon is getting up"—said as if a constant state of affairs—and I am invited to wait in the living room/dining room. It is darkly painted, with antique gold sitting-sofa and chairs, and dark drapes over the tall windows in the bay. The dinner table is set for the family and myself; the center of the table holds a raised plate with some dozen pepper cellars of all sizes and styles. The lighting is stark; the ceiling has been modified to hold spotlights that shine down, casting clear shadows on any character who enters the scene.

Amanda emerges, teen-age daughter. A combination of both parents, totally, implausibly. Then Hermione, younger and smaller, "making eyes" to keep a stranger's attention. Elizabeth returns for chit-chat and some sizing up. Looking for an "in," I say I have come via Negroponte. I try not to be too American, sensing that would be bad, except where I might be a conduit to yet more hardware, tossed off by MIT as too old yet pure gold to Pask's impoverished and sometimes bankruptcy-making research laboratory, situated just below the dining room in his dank basement.

Steps in the upper hallway—sharp, deliberate taps, each step intentional— sound like Gordon's. Now he's coming down the stairs. I see him pass in the hallway and go into the kitchen; then he comes out with purpose and goes right back upstairs. Must have forgotten something. I wait but he does not return for some time. Then the same timed steps down stairs, into the kitchen, and return back up the stairs without break. I try not to notice but after this occurs some five times I look un-committedly toward the family, hoping for a clue. Elizabeth says, "Gordon is doing his rituals" as if to say, "Today is Monday." "Aha," I casually reply. Six times, seven, eight times down the stairs I count, and this time Gordon swings into the dining room with a flourish and says, "How-do, Paul, have a good flight?"

The dinner atmosphere holds a tension, Elizabeth is not happy with something. Surely living with a genius is not easy, I think, but little did I know at the time. Main course, salad, sweet, cheese, savory for Gordon, all made by Elizabeth, yet again tonight. Lots of wine, poured at frequent intervals into all the adults' glasses by Gordon. Each time that he drains his glass, faster than anyone, he refills my glass and Elizabeth's and then his, near to the top. Does he want company, or justification of his own drinking, or all of us drunk?

Dinner finished, the family leaves the table and we talk. The surface is friendly, the undertone demanding. Did I understand his papers? What programming could I do? Was I available to meet with the Admiralty to discuss their needs? Here in his own element, smaller yet more powerful in his Edwardian dining room with high ceilings and ceiling-inset stage lighting, he is elfin, a creature, and not a person *per se*.

His company, System Research, Ltd., had been awarded a contract by a group of research psychologists in the UK Admiralty, as a result of his relationship with research psychologists in the U.S. Army. They all knew that existing approaches to the problems of training and planning were too limited.

They were intrigued (and a bit bewildered) by Pask's "conversation theory," a formal, comprehensive, explanatory framework for harnessing the processes of learning and therefore a strategy to build software interfaces that support it. And that is where I found my place: Purported interlocutor between The Maestro and those interested in applying his ideas. (I could also provide access to America's advanced technological prowess; in that era, technology available in the United Kingdom was 5 years behind that of the United States.) Could entailment meshes be a practical way to improve strategic training systems? Could a re-implementation of THOUGHTSTICKER (Pangaro, 2001) in a sensible (and reproducible, and reliable, and documented) environment provide an advance in capability? Could Pask stay focused on a client's problem long enough to complete a working prototype?

Answering these questions becomes the blueprint for our shared future, but the delays in his appearing for dinner become metaphor for the 10-plus years of collaboration that follow. His staying up all night to work on correspondence, write and re-write papers, and carry on his theoretical work mean that Gordon does not get to bed much before mid- or late morning. So he really did not care to wake up on any schedule (nor could he). Getting him out of bed requires countless reminders and some badgering; alarm clocks are irrelevant, a reliable technology of no use here. (The barbiturates he takes to sleep do not help. Besides, he has to take enough to cancel the amphetamines he takes to work through the day. All the coffee and wine do not seem to make much difference. Only the Perrier matters: It is necessary to flush everything through.)

On my earliest visits I wait for him to get up and come to dinner, engaged in wonderful conversations while getting to know the daughters better. Elizabeth one day suggests that I wake him myself. It is a clever and expedient idea on her part, and now I better understand her tense demeanor. *Of course I am thrilled at the idea of becoming closer to the daily habits of this creature I have chosen to follow.*

I climb the stairs and listen outside the bedroom. The snoring is resonant, clear. I knock and push open the door. The bedroom has tall ceilings, patterned-papered walls, and dark drapes drawn closed against the day's now-waning evening sun. There is a shamble of clothing everywhere. Two small twin beds, impossible to tell which holds The Pask, until the sound of snoring brings my attention to the one on the left.

As my eyes adjust to the dark, I see his tiny frame outlined under the covers. His hair, always a salt-and-pepper fright wig, is matted with sweat. "Gordon," I call, gently at first and then louder until he responds by not snoring. "Gordon, it's time for dinner!" "Oh … what?" I hear his surprise in this unexpected voice disturbing him, one he cannot as easily ignore. He turns, rubs his hair and sits up on the side of the bed, a flat board with no mattress, lying near to the floor. Bedding aside, I see how he sleeps: In socks, briefs, and the white shirt he will wear that day on rising. (Fortunately it is of the wash-and-wear variety and by the time he dons his jacket, it is relatively wrinkle-free.)

We are both a bit embarrassed. I begin to talk about the day and what must come next in the Admiralty contract. This focus is welcome to us both, and lets him awaken the body while his mind is already working fine. In time, over years, this ritual repeats but becomes more difficult. He is less willing; I am less innocent and less patient; he is less patient or more pulled down by the drugs, or both.

FUTURES

The years that follow contain elation, enmity, and uncertainty. On a given day, would Gordon be intuitively compassionate (loaning me US$7,000 in today's money without hesitation) or willfully induce conflict (attacking me in front of sponsors that we both need on our side)? *In our next interaction would he be friendly sprite or probing sorcerer?*

No matter—I could never return to the banal (if predictable) interactions with trivial machines, nor to the fallacious claims of AI.Pask showed me how to live in a coherence of my personal worlds, integrating computer science and cybernetics, coding and opera, description and experience, Winky Dink and *Volare!* My years with him are seductive and challenging, generative and exhausting. I would repeat them, not happily but willfully. *Living in interaction is more like singing and opera than computing and devices.* From unreliable humans to Winky Dink to MIT and its computers and AI, he brought my trajectory full cybernetic circle, back to unreliable human interactions again. If Winky Dink is a comforting illusion of connection and reliability, Pask is a volatile embrace of precariousness and vast, seductive possibility. We may *make sense* through interactions with the physical world, but we *co-create meaning* in our living through interactions with human beings. For me personally, that journey of meaning-making is well portrayed by my interactions with Gordon and best explained by Pask's conversation theory. For me professionally, I use his ideas in every project and interaction design, long after his lifestyle takes him away prematurely (Pangaro, 1996). My future trajectory is made simple, as with any great theory: *In meaning-making every day in the 40 years since meeting Pask, I shall act, and learn, and act again, drawing strength and trust from the coherence I make in my own living.*

REFERENCES

Cariani, P. (2007). To evolve an ear: Epistemological implications of Gordon Pask's electrochemical devices. *Systems Research, 10*(3), 19–33. doi:10.1002/sres. 3850100305

Harris, T. (2016). *How Technology Hijacks People's Minds.* Retrieved December 14, 2017, from http://www.tristanharris.com/2016/05/how-technology-hijacks-peoples-minds%E2%80%8A-%E2%80%8Afrom-a-magician-and-googles-design-ethicist/.

Heims, S. J. (1991). *The Cybernetics Group.* Cambridge, MA: MIT Press.

McCulloch, W. (1970). *Why the mind is in the head. Embodiments of mind.* Cambridge, MA: MIT Press, p 87.

Mentzer, M. (2013). *Winky Dink and You [Video File].* Retrieved from https://www.youtube.com/watch?v=u5TdRhNLOPk

Minsky, M. (1967). *Computation: Finite and infinite machines.* Cambridge, MA: Prentice Hall.

Pangaro, P. (1996). Gordon Pask Obituary. The London Guardian Newspaper, April 16, 1996.

Pangaro, P. (2001). THOUGHTSTICKER: A personal history of conversation theory in software. *Kybernetes, 30*(5/6), 790–806.

Pangaro, P. (2012). *What is cybernetics?* Retrieved December 14, 2017, from https://vimeo.com/pangaro/what-is-cybernetics.

Pangaro, P. (2017). Cybernetics as Phoenix: What ashes, what new life? In L. Werner (Ed.), *Cybernetics: State of the art.* Berlin, Germany: TU.

Papert, S. (1965). Introduction. In W. McCulloch (Ed.), *Embodiments of mind.* Cambridge, MA: MIT Press.

Pask, G. (1961). *An approach to cybernetics.* London, UK: Hutchinson.

Pask, G. (1971). A comment, a case history, and a plan. In J. Reichardt (Ed.), *Cybernetics, art, and ideas.* New York, NY: New York Graphic Society.

Pask, G. (1976). An Outline Theory of Media for Education and Entertainment. *International Conference on Evaluation and Research in Educational Television and Radio,* Open University, April 1976.

Pask, G. (1980). Consciousness. Proceedings 4th European Meeting on Cybernetics and System research, Linz, Austria, March 1978. Journal of Cybernetics, Washington DC: Hemisphere.

Pask, G. (1982). *Microman: Computers and the evolution of consciousness.* London, UK: Macmillan.

Pickering, A. (2015). The Next Macy Conference: A New Interdisciplinary Synthesis, *IEEE Technology and Society Magazine,* September 2015.

Solon, O. (2017). *Ex-Facebook president Sean Parker: Site made to exploit human 'vulnerability'.* Retrieved December 14, 2017, from https://www.theguardian.com/technology/2017/nov/09/facebook-sean-parker-vulnerability-brain-psychology.

Wiener, N. (1948). *Cybernetics: Or control and communication in the animal and the machine.* Paris: Hermann & Cie; Cambridge, MA: MIT Press.

Winky, D., & You. (n.d.). *In Wikipedia.* Retrieved December 14, 2017, from https://en.wikipedia.org/wiki/Winky_Dink_and_You.

Weizenbaum, J. (1976). *Computer power and human reason: From judgment to calculation.* New York, NY: W H Freeman & Co.

Wright Steenson, M. (2017). *Architectural intelligence: How designers and architects created the digital landscape.* Cambridge, MA: MIT Press.

FOR THE LOVE OF CYBERNETICS

PETER D. TUDDENHAM

This narrative is a response to an invitation to share my story regarding cybernetics. I begin with an exploration of what "for the love of cybernetics" means to me. Tracing experiences and connections to cybernetics over the course of 50 years I explore how I observe and give voice to my relation with people and situations both personal and professional. I explore life and how it is enriched by knowing cybernetics. Recent projects to encourage systems and cybernetic literacy building on work with ocean, earth, air, and energy literacies are described.

INTRODUCTION

When Jocelyn Chapman invited me to write about my experience with cybernetics she at first addressed the e-mail to "Lovers of Cybernetics." I had never thought of myself as a "lover" per se of "cybernetics," but as she named me to be one and write about it I started to wonder what it might mean to be a lover of cybernetics. As a lover of cybernetics and with the understanding that one of the tenets of cybernetics is the concept of circularity, naturally I had to find the circularity implicit in the request and consider the cybernetics of lovers as well.

The request produced a plethora of directions to proceed. In the e-mail, Jocelyn referred to the invitation in the subject line as "For the love of cybernetics," which is a nuanced difference, but one that is enough of a distinction to warrant its own interpretation. So now in addition to the first two topics I have stated there is another. From the subject line the obvious circularity is the cybernetics of love. So now I seemed to have at least three topics to consider: (a) A lover of cybernetics, (b) The cybernetics of lovers, and (c) Describing "for the love of cybernetics." And in a further e-mail to the group of invited authors Jocelyn offered the opportunity to follow whatever path of writing that was meaningful to illustrate the richness of the variety of possibilities of the relevance and application of cybernetics to our lives, to society, and to life in general.

I had to think about, and reflect on, what cybernetics has meant to me, as a person, a parent, husband, employee, employer, sailor, skier, learner, musician, singer, glider pilot, photographer, cybernetician, and cybernetist, a systems scientist perhaps, multiple roles at different stages of my life. I also began more reflection of life when I might consider myself a lover. But then I have been a lover of many people and things. How has my knowledge of cybernetics, or the existence of cybernetic principles in the world, influenced me as a lover? Or perhaps how is it reflected in my loving?

I have been surprised by the level of personal introspection and reflection that this request has provoked in me. I have indulged in a journey exploring my understanding of love, and my understanding of cybernetics and then their relation in order to complete this article, and I have come to know cybernetics at its foundation as the study of communication, control, feedback, and organization and the consequences of that study. The study and understanding of those elements or aspects can occur at all levels of existence. Over the years, cybernetics has included the importance, or centrality, of the role of the observer in any description of anything. The observer will describe the observation with the language, symbols, and meaning structures that are embodied in the observer's learning and life experiences. Further adding to this description is the role of the observer, of the observer. For this article I am aware, to an extent, of my observations and writing about love and cybernetics in the different configurations I have described above. Furthermore, those three statements are for me components or markers of the boundary for this article, each one of which evokes a response in emotional, cognitive, and linguistic ways.

As I proceed with this writing I need to consider my own role as an observer of my own observing about these topics when thinking about my relationship with the concept or science or field of cybernetics. My initial understanding of cybernetics was the classic science of communication and control. As love can be thought of as about communication, and control in many dimensions, there is significant value in exploring the personal understanding of, and relation to, love through an understanding of the relation of cybernetics and love. Love affects how we communicate and how our bodies, actions, and language respond to love. When I think about love I am drawn to consider the role of the heart and then the role of the observer of the heart, my heart, and your heart. I am observing here, to start this exploration, with my direct experience of love and cybernetics and their relation, and my heart, and giving voice to that observing here in this article.

I have also found myself in an internal conversation between my head and my heart about love and cybernetics. The heart is often described as the center of love, or that love starts in the heart. Cybernetics on the other hand is more cerebral and is an abstract way of knowing from the brain or head. I have been having this conversation from the heart to the head and back again asking questions. What is the feeling of love? What is the cybernetics of love? One of the first systems I studied in the Open University Systems Behaviour Course T241, in 1979, was the respiratory system or otherwise described as the heart–lung system (Montgomery, 1973). That connection is all about communication and control and regulation, but the texts and studies said nothing about love, or feelings, or emotion and their effect on the heart–lung system.

In order to appreciate these relationships and connections I am also reflecting on the work of others. For example, the work of Humberto Maturana (2008) as described in the *Origin of the Humanness in the Biology of Love*. Maturana's descriptions have a well-respected place in the field of cybernetics. His work puts emphasis on the role of language, and internal language, in the development of relation and the organizational structural closure of the human. I have found his work and joint work with Francesca Varela (Maturana & Varela, 1987) an important factor in the development of my interest in cybernetics.

In a book entitled *The Biology of Love*, Arthur Janov (2000) took a very different perspective from Maturana's approach as he described love as a unified theory of psychology and brain chemistry. The point here is that an understanding of cybernetics enables me to read and hopefully understand phenomena of different types. For example, love, using a way of knowing called cybernetics, involves a more philosophical and natural approach with Maturana and the more physical function level as described by Janov.

Peter Selg's (2012) work to describe sacramental physiology of the heart in his book *The Mystery of the Heart* has potential implications for further study of the human heart and blood system as a cybernetic system. An avenue of research might be entitled the soul of cybernetics or the cybernetic soul. If love comes from the heart then understanding the role and functioning of the heart in love, and in its function as essential for life when studied from the perspective of cybernetics, may provide insight into our being in the cosmos, and perhaps how love and cybernetics may be connected in an explanation.

Another connection between cybernetics, love, and the heart is the term used by Stafford Beer in his book *Heart of Enterprise* (1979). He uses the human being as a model for the description of viability in any organization, which he calls enterprise. What can we learn about viability by looking at love and the heart from the perspective of cybernetics?

SUMMARY OF SOME OF MY PERSONAL EXPERIENCE WITH CYBERNETICS

Before I explore the three themes I identified at the beginning of this article I think it may be helpful to provide my personal history with "cybernetics" to give some context for my discussion. My first experience with the term cybernetics began somewhere between 1969 and 1972 when I was randomly browsing books in a bookshop in Highgate Village in North London near where I went to school. I remember purchasing the book *Psycho-Cybernetics* (Maltz,

1960), which describes approaches to learning about self-image and performance improvement through forms of feedback among other cybernetic ideas. The book was based to some extent on the work of one of the founders of cybernetics, Norbert Weiner (1961). Another influence for me that reinforced my interest in organization, communication, and control (aspects of cybernetics) was the work of Wilfred Brown and Elliott Jacques as described in *Exploration in Management* (1965), which I also purchased as a teenager from the same bookshop. These two books describe different communication patterns in different organizational structures with different purposes and outcomes. Nevertheless, they both illustrated the cybernetic principles in relationships, communication, control, organization, structure, feedback, and the role of the observer observing either him- or herself or observing the behavior and communication of a commercial organization.

I was not to encounter the term "cybernetics" again until I met Professor Bill Reckmeyer at San Jose State University in 1983 when considering pursuing a master's degree in Systems and Cybernetics. He introduced me to the American Society for Cybernetics (ASC). We worked together to use the consensus methodologies created by John Warfield, applying cybernetic principles to design and decision making at the Adolph Coors Company in Golden, Colorado. To read more about Warfield's work see his book, *A Science of Gemeric Design* (1995). In 1986, I met Frank Burns who had started a company in Arlington, Virginia called Metasystems Design Group (MDG). Along with Lisa Kimball and Billye Adams, they were building on Burns' organizational development work in the U.S. Army and on the work of Stafford Beer in *Platform for Change* (1975) and Bandler and Grinder, who were using feedback as described in cybernetics to link a person's internal experience with their language and their patterns of behavior. I subsequently worked with the crew at MDG as they implemented and managed one of the first Internet-based computer conferencing systems, called the MetaNet, using software called Caucus. This work was applying cybernetics in the development of organizations and individuals using technology to support communication and feedback. One of the founding reasons that cybernetics was named as a distinct subject was to examine the developing experiences of man/woman with machines. MDG was experimenting with the role of computer communication networks to support change and innovation in large hierarchical organizations by creating metanetworks.

Between 1986 and 1991, I worked at CAE-Link corporation (formerly Allen and then Singer) as a senior systems scientist. While there I met Paul Pangaro in Washington, D.C. to discuss cybernetics, computer-based learning, and intelligent tutoring systems (2013). He introduced me to his work and the cybernetics and conversation theory of Gordon Pask (1961, 1976) and Harri-Augstein and Thomas (1961). During my time with CAE-Link, I served as guest faculty at the U.S. Army War College as we researched the cognitive, emotional, and leadership characteristics of generals in the U.S. Army. One of the goals of this research was to develop educational and computer technology, along with curriculum and courses to encourage rapid development of emotional and cognitive capabilities required in senior leadership positions. Another cybernetic consideration in our course design was the cybernetic principles of conversation and pattern as described by Gregory Bateson (1972).

As part of my participation with the ASC, I have had conversations on cybernetics with many members. I met with the president of the ASC, Ranulph Glanville, at his house and at the local coffee and cake shop in his home town of Southsea near Portsmouth in England, on visits to my family nearby in southern England. We had several conversations on cybernetics and design and conversation and the behavior and actions of people based on their relation to architectural spaces. He expressed how he came to love cybernetics in an essay called "Going Home: Meeting Gordon Pask." In the essay he describes cybernetics as "Bringing precision, intensity, clarity. I was home." He finished the essay by saying "I now live with the beauty that is cybernetics." A wonderful set of perspectives on his love of cybernetics is compiled in the work *Ranulph Glanville and How to Live the Cybernetics of Unknowing* (Brier, Guddemi, & Kauffman, 2017). I attended one of the last public activities of Ranulph before he died as he organized the ASC 2013 annual conference at the University of Bolton. Here he encouraged the recursive activity of discussing in small groups the relations between Acting–Learning–Understanding by reflecting, collaborating, conversing, and doing.

At that 2013 ASC conference I re-connected with another scholar of cybernetics, Pille Bunnell. I met Pille in Vancouver in the 1990s when exploring the possibility of making connections between her work on the biology of love and my work on ocean science education with the then-named Bermuda Biological Station for Research, now the Bermuda Institute for Ocean Sciences. She and I volunteered to demonstrate a fascinating simulation system that gave the participants the opportunity to experience psychosis and what it might be like to be schizophrenic. This was a multimedia system called Labyrinth Psychotica, Simulating Psychotic Phenomena, which was created by Jennifer Kanary Nikolova. Pille played the role of mother while I played the son as we both engaged with the "doing" of the simulation, and in the spirit of the conference highlighted struggles with acting, learning, and understanding.

Over the past eight years I have also participated in seminars on cybernetics organized by Professor Stuart Umpleby at the George Washington University. The seminars have all been framed in the context of cybernetics and reflexive systems with topics ranging from World Futures on a global scale to group problem structuring and decision making to individual development and recognition of personal purpose. Some of these seminars were video recorded by the College of Exploration and are free to watch at https://vimeo.com/channels/317919.

With that context and brief review of some of the highlights of my encounters with scholars and practitioners of cybernetics, I will make some comments on the five headings that arose from the invitation to write this article. I will offer commentary and some thoughts on my experience or relationship with these ideas in this order: (1) As a lover of cybernetics, (2) As the cybernetics of lovers, and (3) Describing "for the love of cybernetics."

AS A LOVER OF CYBERNETICS

The preceding paragraphs describe in brief outline some of the more significant developments that have kept my interest in cybernetics. Until now I have not thought of myself as a lover of cybernetics. The description demonstrates a continuing interest over the past 45 years or so, but it has not been a central and defining subject or context for my life. The topic has been always present in my thinking and acting, albeit with varying degrees of intensity, awareness, and practical application. While considering the challenge that this article poses I want to make the connection between my knowledge and interest in cybernetics and the love I have for my family and how I came to know, or came to experience, love in my life.

I was fortunate to experience a loving family, which extended to grandparents and uncles, aunts, cousins, and other family members when I grew up in London. My grandparents and uncles and aunts all lived relatively close by in and around London, and we had many opportunities to gather for family events and holidays and vacations. I think from an early age I was always curious about my experiences of love in the actions of those closest to me, and the effects of communications, and of different models of parenting and controlling of behavior.

I observed differences in the relationship patterns of different families of my extended family. The acts of love and compassion and experience to me as a child were of course different depending on the specific relationship. Therefore, it is prudent to be cautious about generalizations about the cybernetics of love.

Perhaps talking about communication and control in a loving relationship might be more directly understood, especially by anyone who has never heard of cybernetics. A lover as a communicator and controller of relation and in a relationship is a possible way to approach thinking about myself as a lover of cybernetics. In the 1980s while an executive in residence at the Center for Ethics at Arizona I was introduced to the work of William T. Powers who developed Control Theory in Psychology. See https://www.amazon.com/William-T.-Powers/e/B001IC9C2G for a list of his books.

THE CYBERNETICS OF LOVERS

Throughout history, lovers' words and actions have been the source of rich stories, plays, films, performances, and poems, to name just a few.

For the first 26 years of my life I lived in the British language culture in England, and for the past 37 I have lived in the American language culture in the United States. It is interesting if not surprising to read the difference in description of the word lover presented by U.S.-based dictionary.com (Dictionary.com, n.d.) where the first definition of lover is "a person who is in love with another" whereas the first definition offered from the UK-based Oxford Dictionary (Oxford Dictionaries, n.d.) for the word lover is "A partner in a sexual or romantic relationship outside marriage." This example illustrates to an extent the problem, or the "promiscuity" I think Glanville described it, of language.

Another explanation of this phrase could be how we understand the word "lover" in different cultures. In the United States it may refer more to the behavior, the communication and control of one person in relation to another in a loving relationship, whereas in the United Kingdom it may be more about the behavior patterns and communications of one person in a marriage having a sexual or romantic relationship outside of marriage and all the different actions and feedbacks and observations and cultural and societal reactions to the situation. This example highlights my interest in the topic of cybernetics as a frame for examining assumptions and understandings and illustrates the nuance of language that exists embedded in cultural and linguistic traditions.

DESCRIBING "FOR THE LOVE OF CYBERNETICS"

This is possibly the intent of this series of articles on cybernetics. Until I was put in the category of someone who could talk about love and cybernetics, I had not associated my behavior or interests by relating cybernetics and love. Cybernetics enables a disciplined way to study "form, pattern, purpose, organization, and so on" as Gregory Bateson (1991, p. 307) says in the "Last Lecture." Whether I want to study the cosmos, the solar system, ocean-earth-air-energy-life systems, corporate organization, family systems, development of living plants and animals, art and theater, Nano particles or consciousness, the language and discipline of cybernetics provides doors and pathways, philosophies, methods, and tools with which to explore that territory. For that reason, I have to re-affirm my interest, and perhaps love, for cybernetics.

I have applied my understanding of cybernetics as a "platform for change" (Beer, 1975) as in the United States we have developed a series of collaboratively designed and collectively agreed on guides to ocean, earth science, atmospheric science, energy, and climate literacy.

In 2002 my organization, the College of Exploration, worked with the National Geographic Society (NGS) to link oceanography with geography as a path to ocean literacy. Building on work completed by the NGS in 1994 we created a scope and sequence chart that mapped national geography standards to key ocean concepts. We created a metasystem to bring together geographers, oceanographers, and educators to create the "Oceans for Life" document (2003).

This work and that of many others resulted in my engagement in similar and larger efforts in the United States to bring together scientists, educators, and policy makers in projects to create guides for Ocean Literacy in 2004

(Cava, Schoedinger, Strang, & Tuddenham, 2005) and then Earth Science Literacy in 2009 (Wysession et al., 2012). These works, combined with similar work for Atmospheric Literacy, Energy Literacy, and Biological Literacy, are providing some foundations for work on systems and cybernetic literacy.

There is still much work to do to see more understanding of the potential from studying life and nature through the lens of cybernetics and systems. In 2009, we started a similar effort to create a cybernetics and systems literacy guide, which stalled in 2010 for lack of funding support (Tuddenham, 2008). Now I am engaged with the International Society for the Systems Sciences as President-elect (2018–2019), the International Federation for Systems Research (Edson, Metcalf, Tuddenham, & Chroust, 2017), The International Council on Systems Engineering, the International Society for Systems Pathologies, and members of the American Society of Cybernetics to re-energize the development of a guide for systems and cybernetic literacy (Tuddenham, 2017). The challenge with this project is the significant range of interpretations of the word "system" or "systems" and the relation of systems theory and systems science to cybernetics. For example Ray Ison, in his book *Systems Practice: How to Act* (2017), has "a model of some of the different influences that have shaped contemporary systems approaches and the lineages from which they emerged," which places cybernetics toward the description of systems as epistemologies. He lists 20 subject areas that have influenced over 25 different cyber-systemic approaches in different settings. The work in ocean literacy and earth science literacy produced between seven and nine big ideas or principles. The work to create a guide for cyber-systems literacy is continuing.

REFLECTIONS

The request to write this article has prompted me to think about and feel about my relation to cybernetics, even my love of cybernetics. As authors, we were encouraged to indulge our interests and pursue a path of personal exploration and commentary. I appreciate that this writing has been a stream of consciousness and has gone in several different directions. I hope that by sharing some highlights of my discovery of cybernetics and my explorations in life that have considered many of the different perspectives on what cybernetics is and means will be helpful to others. I hope that the three sub-headings are prompts for further explorations, investigations, and scientific and artistic creations and discoveries.

REFERENCES

ASC. (2013). *2013 ASC Annual Conference*. Retrieved from http://asc-cybernetics.org/2013/

Bateson, G. (1972). *Steps to an ecology of mind*. Chicago, IL: University of Chicago Press.

Bateson, G. (1991). *Sacred unity: Further steps to an ecology of mind.* New York, NY: Harper Collins.

Beer, S. (1975). *Platform for change.* Chichester, UK: John Wiley.

Beer, S. (1979). *The heart of enterprise.* Bath, UK: Wiley.

Brier, S., Guddemi, P., & Kauffman, L. (2017). *Ranulph Glanville and how to live the cybernetics of unknowing.* Exeter, England: Imprint Academic.

Brown, W. (1965). *Exploration in management.* London, UK: Penguin.

Cava, F., Schoedinger S., Strang, C., & Tuddenham, P. (2005). Science content and standards for ocean literacy: A report on ocean literacy. Retrieved from http://www.coexploration.org/oceanliteracy/documents/OLit2004-05_Final_Report.pdf

Dictionary.com. (n.d). Retrieved from http://www.dictionary.com/browse/lover

(2017). Edson, M., Metcalf, G., Tuddenham, P., & Chroust, G. *Systems literacy.* Linz, Austria: Johannes Kepler University.

Harri-Augstein, S., & Thomas, L. (1961). *Learning conversations.* London, UK: Routledge.

Ison, R.L. (2017). *Systems practice: How to act.* London, UK: Springer.

Janov, A. (2000). *The biology of love.* Amherst, MA: Prometheus Books.

Maltz, M. (1960). *Psycho-cybernetics.* New York, NY: Penguin.

Maturana, H. (2008). *The origin of the humaness of the biology of love.* Charlottesville, VA: Imprint Academic.

Maturana, H., & Varela, F. (1987). *The tree of knowledge: The biological roots of human understanding.* Boston, MA: Shambhala Publications.

Montgomery. (1973). *Systems Behaviour: Module 7 Units 13/14, The Human Respiratory System.* Milton Keynes: The Open University Press.

Oceans for Life. (2003). *National Geographic Society,* Washington DC: Author.

Oxford Dictionaries. (n.d.). Retrieved from https://en.oxforddictionaries.com/definition/lover

Pangaro, P. (2013). *Cybernetics defintion.* Retrieved from http://www.pangaro.com/definition-cybernetics.html

Pask, G. (1961). *An approach to cybernetics.* New York, NY: Harper and Brothers.

Pask, G. (1976). *Conversation theory.* New York, NY: Elsevier Scientific. doi:10.1093/sw/22.1.69-b

Selg, P. (2012). *The mystery of the heart.* Great Barrington, MA: Steiner Books.

Tuddenham, P. (2008). *The college of exploration and "Systems" literacy.* Retrieved from http://www.coexploration.org/systemsliteracy/

Tuddenham, P. (2017). *Systems literacy.* Retrieved from http://www.systemsliteracy.net

Warfield, J. (1995). *A science of generic design: Managing complexity through systems design.* Ames, IA: Iowa State University Press.

Weiner, N. (1961). *Cybernetics or control and communication in the animal and the machine.* New York, NY: John Wiley.

Wysession, M. E., LaDue, N., Budd, D. A., Campbell, K., Conklin, M., Kappel, E., … & Tuddenham P. (2012). Developing and applying a set of earth science literacy principles. *Journal of Geoscience Education, 60,* 95–99.

HACK OR DIE: HOW HUMANITY STEERS INTO ITS POST-DIGITAL FUTURE

Lucas Pawlik

This article introduces stories as a link between culture and evolution. It elaborates how the decline of interhuman communication leads to a loss of perception, capability for cooperation, and human intelligence and contributes to the current ecocide. It shows how cybernetics hacked the relationship between evolution and machine development, which brought forth the outlines of man's current digital transformation and future. It suggests that Lucas Pawlik is still working on a possible sustainable future for humanity that Heinz von Foerster tried to initiate.

In Love and Appreciation

For Barbara Vogl, Marshall McLuhan, Heinz, Tom and Madeline von Foerster.

For Those Who Allow Me to Lay my Ear on the Track of History.

For Those Who Hack(ed) The World, and For the Greatest Human Technologies:

Imagination and Communication.

OUR HUMAN STORY: THE ORIGINAL CAUSAL FEEDBACK CHAIN OF HUMAN ORGANIZATION

From 1946 to 1953, the world's leading intelligence closed ranks to understand and design circular causal feedback patterns in humans, in nature, and in machines; these seemingly disparate realms were investigated, modeled, and probed *in vitro* and *in vivo*. These people, geniuses from the most diverse fields, many with achievements beyond the scope of a single book or paper, came to recognize themselves as cyberneticians. In their goal-oriented conversations, they started to hack the patterns' connections, the social steering of humanity, and the working of its minds with the evolution of our biosphere, founding the basis for humanity's future organization. How could one understand, communicate, and steer this development? The last survivors of this group agreed on a surprisingly simple statement: stories were the primary medium of human organization (Bateson, 2002, p. 12; Foerster, 2003, p. 294).

The extraordinary attempt to understand, model, calculate, and steer life through causality identifying patterns of goals and causes from the perspective of a reflective, historical decision-making organism had its foundation in Aristotle's life work. In pursuing this perspective in theory and practice, he laid the foundation for Western cultures and sciences, ranging from physics, biology, ethics, and economics to medicine, mathematics, and ways of governing states.

Aristotle was also the first to recognize the story as a causal feedback model, both imitating and reorganizing human behavior through its unity of actions/results (mythos/plot) and its effect on audiences by the specific values it expresses (Aristoteles, 2011, p. 10) The structure of human stories, from their beginning through their middle part to their end, forms one circular causal feedback loop. An inciting incident, an initial event (A), sets the story in motion, which, via progressive complications, unfolds in circular patterns of actions and results (B) to arrive at a final resolution A (McKee, 2005, p. 199). Through the invention and perception of causes and goals, goals become causes, leading to new goals. As one story ends and another begins, we create human history because of ourselves and in spite of ourselves. Aristotle's interest in stories (myths), however, focused on the analysis of Greek theater in its transition from an oral to a literate, linear-hierarchical structure to understand, sustain, and further this progress (Aristoteles, 2011, p. 7). The mythological essence of stories, with emotionally loaded impressions and experiences and a heightened presence transcending space and time, inward and outward reality (Cassirer, 1994, p. 45–49)—reaching back to the origins of language and consciousness and relating us to our evolutionary ancestors—became only graspable through a cybernetic perspective in which time–space and realities are understood as constructions of our nervous systems (Foerster 2003). Picture an early human, being alarmed by noise in a hunting situation: he has to imagine/ decide from a few intense momentary impressions, jumping between present, pasts, and futures and judging the situation. Steering our lives in such a manner, we search for possibilities within constraints, we answer a principally undecidable question (Foerster, 2003, p. 293) —"What's the story?"—to model and enact our future, steering our personal life as well as history (Foerster, 2003, p. 294). Our stories create our characters, our values, and our goals.

Just as metaphors link different systems of our brain and nervous system, stories link causal patterns of actions within their imagined and observed environment. Actions, changes, and further adaptive/creative acting bring forth a development that unites actors (humans, machines, organisms) through stories with their environment through time (Bateson, 2002, pp. 12–15). From the cybernetic perspective ("cybernetic" being derived from the Greek word for "steering"), all biological forms and machines are systems made up of circular causal feedback patterns. Human stories and communication allow us to steer our steering, as we compute multiple possible chains of events to act toward the future we desire.

> My finger goes smoothly over the unchanged surface until I encounter the edge of the white spot. At that moment in time, there is a discontinuity, a step; and soon after, there is a reverse step as my finger leaves the spot behind. This example, which is typical for all sensory experience, shows how our sensory system—and surely the sensory systems of all other creatures (even plants?) and the mental systems behind the senses (i.e., those parts of the mental systems inside the creatures)—can only operate with events, which we can call changes. The unchanging is imperceptible unless we are willing to move relative to it. (Bateson, 2002, p. 90)

As organisms, we coevolve with our environment by acting on our reflections of how we are doing so. Stories are models of our acting, in which we develop patterns of culture and nature, as they emerge through our own behavior. We coordinate our internal movement, our imagination, and our way of thinking with our external movement through the perceived patterns of change we previously induced through our actions. To function and prosper, all our language games we develop and practice are part of the story we tell ourselves to enact our living.

The individual organism as well as humanity itself organize themselves through the enactment of their goals and stories, causing our present and future history. Until now, we have largely understood storytelling and language as an abstract semantic phenomenon. If we understand stories as forms of biological feedback, preceding literate and even oral cultures, we will understand the pattern of these changes, the history of human organization as part of our evolution, as organisms related to the evolution of our planet. This is important, because we primarily evolved through interhuman communication and interaction in coordinating our emotions and intentions and our creative adaption to our environment. We need to learn and practice human-to-human communication with its verbal and nonverbal modes and cues. The lack of these interhuman communication/interaction leads to a corruption of language, dramatically decreasing our cognitive-empathic ability to sense and relate to ourselves and others: The world seems to be in the grip of a fast-spreading disease which by now has assumed almost global dimensions. In the individual, the symptoms manifest themselves by a progressive corruption of his or her faculty to perceive, with corrupted language being the pathogen (i.e., the agent that makes the disease so highly contagious). Worse in progressive stages of this disorder, the afflicted become numb, they become less and less aware of their affliction (Foerster, 2003).

Foerster describes this process as trivialization, as a decay of perception and communication, as an industrialized process of humanity's digitalization. A trivial machine is characterized by a one-to-one relationship between its "input" (stimulus, cause) and its "output" (response effect). Increasingly, lacking the encounter of earlier cultures, we engage with each other as living objects whose purpose it is to enable the production of further products and services. In industrialized transformation, the daily interactions of humans become recontextualized as services of predesigned patterns to be consumable as products. Human society becomes a commodity of abstract markets (Polanyi, 1994). In turning from industrialization to digitalization, we begin to model human complexity after our digital machines' fast, but simplistic, effective, but inflexible programs (Foerster, 2003). Correspondingly, international studies on the collaboration of work places show that those who manage our cooperation spend 20–30% of their time dealing with conflicts (Peel, 2013). This recycling patterns of trivialization, in which causes become effects and then causes again, generate a "castration of language," as objectifying ourselves becomes our second nature and we predominantly understand and perceive ourselves through the description of self-objectifying others (Foerster, 2003). We use language to determine our thoughts and experience, instead of practicing to express them, which results in an increasing incapability to freely associate, to conceive change, and to perceive/imagine a future we actually desire (Foerster, 2003). The global decline of human intelligence, especially the recent decline of learned intelligence in highly industrialized countries (Lynn & Harvey, 2008), and its relation to trivialization/digitalization should also be investigated in this regard. The original cyberneticians were aware of the danger of their accomplishments; they knew that "the social misuse of the physical sciences may block or greatly delay any further progress in civilization" (Pias, 2003/I, p. 29). Today's transformation of humanity into a mass that primarily lives for/through the consumption of digitally designed products and pattern of behavior—which enforces an ever-faster lifestyle of decision making and executing—only makes sense in the context of the digital transformation from an industrialized literate culture resulting in Earth's urbanization. The effects and agents of our new electronically enhanced environments pervade and assimilate the former natural environment, human cognition and communication alike. Our social adaptation to the Internet as a new medium of human organization and its technological extensions of body, mind, and senses—automatic navigation systems, smartphones, tablets, smart bombs, self-steering cars, robots, drones—pervade every domain of human activity. This lifestyle increasingly forces global city dwellers to allow all their fundamentals of living to be governed by machine intelligence, from dating to health care, from education to civil infrastructure, from online banking to automated warfare. Part of our mistrust in digitalization comes from the intuitive knowledge that it is part of human history, the story of an economic war game, enacted narratives of conquest and control (Graeber, 2011). This is why we, when we fear machine intelligence, fear it as an elongation of our industrialized war-driven culture. We fear the cultural road we have taken, in which industrialization and digitalization immerse us deeper and deeper in a non-living artificial environment and neglect that the laboratories we enclose ourselves in are part of a bigger laboratory, our evolving biosphere.

We also oversee that cybernetic digitalization marks an endeavor for an organic turn in our sciences. Cybernetics set out to steer the circular causal interrelationship of organisms and their environment, modeling them as goal-oriented feedback loops (Foerster, 2003; Pias, 2004/II, p. 21). Its approach was that you could steer everything to the degree that you could build models of it. (Pias, 2004/II, p. 22). From an industrialized perspective, omnipresent digital computers are the most eminent result, but for the cyberneticians they were just one model in the exploration of the coevolution of organisms and machines. The cybernetician I met and became friends with saw himself as a biological computer in a living biosphere (Foerster, 1999). He calculated himself in as an observer, observing other observers with their own patterns, behaviors, goals, and means (Foerster, 2003).

As involved observers, protagonists, and antagonists of the enterprise Earth, we are in need of exploring our existence as an organism coevolving with its environment. Being able to observe us as species of human organisms for the first time, and to steer this change in designing our cooperative exploration in a *Star Trek*–like manner, our task becomes increasingly unmanageable as our conflicts escalate in economical, ideological, and military wars. Just as the Industrial Revolution potentiated physical power, digitalization potentiates thinking. We are detectives in a science fiction investigation on the tracks of the information age, who are in danger of failing to acknowledge the most transformative tool we encountered in the evolution of the biosphere on which both are based: human imagination. Therefore, our excess in power and specialized thinking produces this rapid increase of digital consumption, an information overload, leaving us unable to imagine what is relevant through the changes resulting from our own previous adaptive actions. We perpetuate war and compete for the increase and control of production, while humanity's primary task is self-organization. Design is our survival, just like exploration is. To survive humanity's digitalization we must inevitably change our industrialized perspective of succeeding by winning wars and dominating the competition for mass products and services. The overall ecocide brought about by this rapid lifestyle entails multiple causes for possible human extinction and threatens our biosphere, the multi-organism we live in:

> Earth's biodiversity—the number of microorganisms, plants, and animals, their genes, and their ecosystems—is declining at an alarming rate, even faster than the last mass extinction 65 million years ago. In fact, two thirds of the terrestrial species that exist today are estimated to be extinct by the end of this century. (Earth's Biodiversity, 2011)

Additionally, the ecocide we cause in our oceans might be even more deadly. Thus, while designing and exploring might sound luxurious and adventurous, it is a matter of survival. Noticing the destruction of our biosphere, our declining human communication and intelligence, we have to ask ourselves: What's our story? To thrive or to die? Self-transformation or self-extinction?

If we want to co-steer the evolution of our biosphere on Earth, we have to model our own evolutionary design through our explorations. From the steering of the brain to the steering of the world, this attempt has for decades been undertaken along very different approaches under the name of cybernetics.

THE ENGINEERS WHO HACKED THE WORLD: HOW THE REVERSE ENGINEERING OF OUR NERVOUS SYSTEM TURNED OUR WORLD INTO A BIOLOGICAL COMPUTER LAB

We live in many realities but in only one world. Everyone is part of its steering. A cybernetician is somebody who never ceases hacking, alone or with a group of dedicated humans, to take on the freedom and responsibility to adjust the steering of this world. Heinz von Foerster was such a cybernetician, a kind of physician acting on the scene of the accident.

He was once asked from which death he would want to save humanity. "From brain death! From brain death! Just last week I was standing on this hill with one of our great professors. He asked me: 'Heinz, do you think computers will ever surpass human intelligence?' 'Definitely!—If humans decide to become more and more stupid, soon computers will outdo them'" (Foerster & Freund, 1992). Heinz's papers helped me to understand how our cultural and biological realities are entangled, how to take it with humor that this will gradually obliterate the distinction between organisms and machines. Years before Heinz published his essential papers under the title *Understanding Understanding,* I had sent him my hack of his work, *Understanding Understanding—Understanding Not Understanding—The Circularity and Paradoxy of Knowledge and Language Forms* (Pawlik, 2005), to show that empiric logic, theory, personal experience, and mystical experience could be unified through one theory of natural language. I hated mathematics and machines. Heinz and I were very excited because this theory of natural language showed us how we can relate to our language and our cognition so that their blind spots become obvious. We learned to understand how we do not understand. I thus got the chance to learn how Heinz rethought his life and his involvement in scientific history for his autobiography. Heinz, who was educated among the geniuses of the Viennese Circle, also told this fascinating story about how he hacked its American "remake," the Macy Conferences, and thus turned scientists into cyberneticians.

One of these future cyberneticians', John von Neumann's, digitalization had already had a first world-changing effect before the conferences had even started. Von Neumann formalized human decision-making behavior in a mathematical control theory (Neumann, 2004). He had built a computer to calculate the critical mass for the first atom bomb to prevent the world from the terrors of Hitler and Stalin (Pias, 2004/II, p. 55). Its future result would be the control/game theory guided by the Cold War's delicate balance of terror that transformed the human military war game into a subgame for the digitalized control of global human behavior. In this game of narratives and numbers, calculated economic destabilization became paramount, military intervention secondary (Pias, 2004/II).

Although digitalization still runs on Neumann's architecture, Neumann was just one of the multidisciplinary geniuses of the New York Macy Conferences, where the European intellectual elite, who had fled from World War II, gathered with the American elite to re-explore and redesign the relationship between human mind, nature, and machines in the 1940s and 1950s. Norbert Wiener, who had invented a mathematically behavioral analysis for steering organisms, machines, and semantic systems, took the leading role (Wiener, Rosenblueth, & Bigelow, in Pias, 2004/II, p. 24). Norbert Wiener had formalized the neuro-physiologist Arturo Rosenblueth's empiric data of the nervous system regaining its dynamic balance from an epileptic stroke as cybernetics and the control and communication in animals and machines via time-delayed feedback (Foerster & Broecker, 2002, p. 334). Wiener's formalization of feedback enabled computers to perform functions that could only be performed by the human brain until then (Pias, 2004/II, p. 399). Digitalization is based on the transfer of self-regulating neurological feedback patterns into highly idealized if-then-repeat-until feedback patterns of machines.

The Macy Conferences were also an incubator for perhaps even more outstanding inventions and cooperation, like the first modeling of human-like machine intelligence by Warren McCulloch and Walter Pitts. They showed in their "logical calculus immanent in the nervous system" that any behavior put in logically unambiguous finite words could be calculated by an appropriate net of artificial nerve cells as elementary computers (Neumann, in Pias, 2004, p. 54).

Claude Shannon, for example, contributed the information theory and its related basis of mathematical cryptography for today's information age and present excitement about distrust-based crypto-currencies and block-chain technology as possible game changers in digital transformation. All in all, there were too many inventors and inventions to mention them in this context.

The key problem of the Macy Conferences was business communication itself, and the best their participants could hope for was to conceptualize the goals and problems in the American attempt to create a new metascience, as the Viennese Circle had tried before them (Pias, 2004/I, p. 29). How to agree on a steering system that steers all steering systems?

The participants finally agreed on a common denominator in the wake of an intervention by the newcomer Heinz von Foerster. The previously unknown Viennese had originally been invited for inventing the first theory and fitting data on human forgetting, based on the circular feedback of molecular and quantum computation (Foerster & Broecker, 2002, pp. 328–329). Already quietly envisioning a better model for computation without a memory, but barely speaking English, he was accepted into the group and made editor of the proceedings. He reluctantly agreed, but claimed he could not pronounce the conference title, "Circular, causal, and feedback mechanisms in biological and social systems" (Pias, 2004/II, p. 47). He suggested "Cybernetics" as the unifying concept and title. This was accepted with laughter, first for the specific conference, then as a title for all conferences. The Macy scientists became cyberneticians, and the newborn science evolved. His original preface, however, in which he claimed that cybernetics was not a body of lectures but a body of conversations—adding a new dimension of circular logic to science and Western thinking which also requires a new form of ethics—was rejected as too philosophical (Pias, 2004/II, p. 48).

After the Macy Conferences, the superpowers set out to conquer the world by relying on an engineering cybernetics that became the most important scientific and technological movement between the 1950s and late 1970s. It promised total control over complex, nonlinear processes from biological to social systems and was even considered a potential neoreligious foundation by communist regimes (Krieg, 2005). Its game plan was that within a unified cultural environment humans, involved in their particular tasks and games, could be steered like ants. Society could be steered like a trivial machine determined by only two feedbacks: the desire to play and the desire to win (Herbert Simon, in Weizenbaum, 1976, p. 260). Finally, this approach dissolved back into traditional sciences and created new neurosciences and computer sciences as well as an ambitious military-funded robotics and artificial intelligence (Krieg, 2005). Heinz, however, united a second transdisciplinary group to explore, model, and understand the relation of machines, language, and human evolution as second-order cybernetics in his Biological Computer Lab (BCL) from 1958 to 1976, until it was no longer possible to do nonmilitary related research due to the Mansfield Amendment (Umpleby, 2003).

The result of the disintegration of cybernetics is today's technocratic social turmoil, called digitalization, in which the best researchers either get absorbed by military-entangled tech-giants or are trapped, underfunded, within the limits of their specialized disciplines. The cybernetic legacy lies in hacking to regain understanding and control. The alternatives are a functioning totalitarian control system, a global war, and/or ecocide.

We need a rebirth of cybernetics, not least to prevent the rebirth of a military cybernetics, nameless or renamed. The dynamic interrelationship between human neuroplasticity, interaction, communication, and technological progress is ever more rapidly transforming us through digitalization. The engineers have already hacked our world. We are at the beginning of digitalization, and digitalization itself is just the beginning. Today's biosphere, society, and humanity itself have become a global BCL. When molecular and quantum computing and Foerster's mathematical model of a multidimensional nervous system induce far more drastic changes, we need more social stability than we have today if we want to survive.

Those who hack(ed) the world must come together to learn from cybernetics how to avoid ecocide and/or human extinction in a war due to a breakdown of human communication and cooperation. To do so, we need new BCL-like research and learning labs to steer our future through and beyond digitalization.

HACK THE MUFFIN: TRANSDISCIPLINARY, TRANSCULTURAL, TRANSGENERATIONAL, AND TRANS-SPECIES: SOCIAL HACKING FOR DIGITAL LEARNING PIONEERS

To tackle today's ecocide and intelligence loss due to our decay in communication, I adapted cybernetics from teaching at the university to use it for social hacking, thus serving cybernetics' original task of co-steering the changes of digitalization. In my co-learning partnership with the Smart-City expert Urska S. Peceny, from the National Aeronautics and Space Administration (NASA) Space Apps Vienna, we invited pioneers from diverse fields, using our pattern recognition and communication skills to link businesses, parents, kids, and organizations alike. Our aim was to foster networks and agents of a sustainable biotechnological future. Together with the entrepreneur and eco visionary Vesela Tanaskovic (2018), who invented a possible solution for an afforestation of the Sahara, the cybernetic education expert Bernard Scott, a pioneer from von Foerster's original Biological Computer Lab, and the digital learning team of the Davinci Lab, we hacked the high-tech grown-up NASA Space Apps Hackathon. With their help, we supported youngsters (10–14 years old) with their business pitches, video design, coding, and robotics to present their solutions for our future (Starc-Peceny, Ovin, & Maček, 2017; NASA Space App Challenge, 2015).

We were allowed to do so because one year earlier we had already shown that kids were interested to turn the ongoing scientific research on ecological development and city design into a participative co-learning game (NASA Space App Challenge, 2016). In our "Biosphere Babies Hack" we used current Earth data to envision the ecological redesign of Earth's biosphere into as a strategy-learning game. In this game players could build ecospheres matching the needs of global cities as biosphere babies to be fed. A biosphere design for a city on Mars as background made the idea of designing ecosystems as a strategy game graspable. We learned from Mars to think like organisms from Earth. The youngsters were eager to engage: "So we could play an online community game exploring how nature and technology work together? Where can I download it? Could you send me the link?"

Liya (one of the young leaders of NASA's first Junior Hackathon in Vienna): "For adults it's easy to say the future will be fine, because they won't live in it. It's me, who'll have to explain to my kids, why the forests are gone, all these species died out, and everything is polluted. We kids are angry, scared, check out from social life to live in our smart phones. Adults pretend everything is fine. All the smart kids want to learn hacking. We're trapped in the Digital Stone Age and want to hack our way out of it."

Lucas: "I really try to change things, but we would have to rewrite the history of cybernetics. That's what got us into this mess in the first place, and most answers are buried there, too. But, what do I know about hacking? It's impossible!"

Liya (laughing): "You told us that the original hackers invented cybernetics to steer the world! That's hacking!—See, I'm twelve in a world full of smart-phone zombies and analog dinosaurs. Against all odds, I'm student representative of my school. Why? Mostly, because I baked muffins for everyone and brought them to the elections. See, every hacking starts with this conversation in your head. Just do what you have to do and tell them the right story! Hacking is not about the digital. You said, true learning means to change who we are and how we live. Cybernetics is the past. Now we can learn most things with computers by ourselves. What we really need is teachers like you, so adults and schools won't get in our way. Otherwise, we're too busy hacking our schools. Please, Lucas! Let's do what seems impossible! We've got to find a way to hack this muffin!"

Children are natural born hackers of the adult's world, eager to take on responsibility. Starting with themselves and their interaction with their parents, they are detectives, who burst with neural and behavioral plasticity, through which they ask: "What's our story on planet Earth? What the hack can we do?" Like cyberneticians, they are ready to explore life itself, to participate in the steering and design of humanity. While knowing that recycling, what we want to conserve, is necessary, this clearly is not enough. If we are interested in our survival in the BCL of our biosphere, we must learn that our kids are already the change we thrived to see in this world. Instead of schooling them, we need to collaboratively explore how to design our future together. From the ongoing history of cybernetics, we need to learn that the systems to do so have yet to be invented by ourselves. I have pondered a long time what Liya meant when she said: The answer I came up with, is that like them I have an appreciative disregard for all system of rules—for in order to create our future our present has to be hacked.

How The Viennese Hacked the Muffin:

There he was, this little Nernst, standing in front of us, and he said: Ladies and Gentlemen, I have made it my aim to free the universe from the heat death! This little man in the auditorium of the University of Vienna wants to change the universe! So he turned back to his chalkboard, wrote down all the physical formulas, changed a couple of parameters, and the universe was liberated. At this moment I understood what science is (Foerster & Freund, 1992).

REFERENCES

Aristoteles (2011). *Poetik*. Berlin, Germany: Akademie Verlag.

Bateson, G. (2002). *Steps to an ecology of mind*. Chicago, IL: University of Chicago Press.

Cassirer, E. (1994). *Philosophie der symbolischen Formen*. 5 vols. Darmstadt: Wissenschaftliche Buchgesellschaft.

Earth's biodiversity: What do we know and where are we headed? (2011). *American Journal of Botany*. www.sciencedaily.com/releases/2011/03/110310173208.htm (accessed January 27, 2018).

Foerster, H. (1999). *2 mal 2 ist Grün*. Cologne, Germany: Suppose Verlag.

Foerster, H. (2003). *Understanding understanding*. New York, NY: Springer Verlag.

Foerster, H., & Broecker, M. (2002). *Teil der Welt. Fraktale einer Ethik. Ein Drama in drei Akten*, Heidelberg, Germany: Carl-Auer Verlag.

Foerster, H., & Freund, S. (1992). Heinz von Foerster. *Cyber-Ethics: A Portrait*. https://www.youtube.com/watch?v=PeE9eAoT6x8&list=RDPeE9eAoT6x8&t=280 (accessed January 27, 2018).

Graeber, D. (2011). *Debt. The First 5000 Years*. New York, NY: Melville House Publishing.

Krieg, P. (2005). The human face of cybernetics: Heinz von Foerster and the history of a movement that failed. *Kybernetes. The International Journal of Systems and Cybernetics*, *34*(3/4), 551–557. doi:10.1108/03684920510581729

Lynn, R., & Harvey, J. (2008). The decline of the world's IQ. *Intelligence*, *36*(2), 112–120. doi:10.1016/j.intell.2007.03.004

McKee, R. (2005). *Story. Substance, structure and principles of screenwriting*. New York, NY: Harper Collins.

NASA Space App Challenge (2015/16). *Biosphere babies—junior challenge*. https://2016.spaceappschallenge.org/mission-reports (accessed January 27, 2018).

Neumann, J. (2004). *Theory of games and economic behavior*. Princeton, NJ: Princeton University Press

Pawlik, L. (2005). *Verstehen Verstehen Nicht-Verstehen Verstehen*. Hollabrunn, Austria: Presshaus Sonnberg

Peel, H. R. (2013). *Whitepaper*. Building a Collaborative Workplace. www.peelhr.com.au/LiteratureRetrieve.aspx?ID=139221 (accessed January 27, 2018).

Pias, C. (2004). *Cybernetics – Kybernetik (The Macy-Conferences 1946–1953). 1 vols.* Zurich & Berlin, Germany: Diaphanes.

Polanyi, K. (1994). *The great transformation*. Boston, MA: Beacon Press.

Starc-Peceny, U., Ovin, R., & Maček, A. (2017). Management of cities and regions. In V. Bobek (Ed.), *Evolution of marketing in smart cities through the collaboration design* (pp. 19–31). Rijeka, Croatia: Intech.

Umpleby, S. (2003). Heinz von Foerster and the Mansfield Amendment. *Cybernetics & Human Knowing*, *10*(3–4), 161–163.

Tanaskovic, V. (2018). *Green-Sahara*. http://veselatanaskovic.com/green-sahara/ (accessed January 27, 2018).

Weizenbaum, J. (1976). *Computer power and human reason. From judgement to calculation*. New York, NY: W.H. Freeman and Company.

MY SCHOLARLY LIFE IN CYBERNETICS

KLAUS KRIPPENDORFF

This article narrates how I discovered cybernetics, who inspired me to make the contributions of which I am proud, and the ideas that led me to recognize the importance of understanding the social world we live in as a consequence of what we do in language. It took me some time before I recognized that circular causality and digitalization that made cybernetics the driver of the current revolution toward a computationally autonomous information society had serious limitations. When used to explain human involvements, the mathematics of cybernetics trivializes what we do to each other and blinds us to recognize how cybernetics transformed society. Studying conversations and discourses made me aware of how cybernetic vocabularies, guiding concepts, and computational metaphors were enacted. By contrast to (first- or second-order) cybernetics, I learned that a cybernetics that is practiced in conversations and acknowledges the social consequences of what it generates had to be reflexive. Shifting attention from causal circularities to reflexive circularities opens up huge new areas for exploring socially meaningful contributions and criticizing the epistemologies of mindless discursive practices (e,g., of claiming the superiority of artificial intelligence and the power of computers). Such claims merely entrap their believers into inaction.

INITIAL EXPOSURE

From 1954 to 1960, I studied at the Hochschule für Gestaltung Ulm, an avant-garde university of design, which opened in 1953 and closed in 1968. I was blessed to be in the midst of an exciting experiment. For me, the most influential teachers were Max Bense, a philosopher who, building on Shannon's

---

Color versions for one or more of the figures in the article can be found online at www.tandfonline.com/GWOF.

theory, was developing an information esthetics, anticipating one rarely understood cultural implication of the digital age, and Horst Rittel, a mathematician, who expanded our horizon by introducing us to system theory, planning theory, game theory, team work, and cybernetics. Cybernetics allowed us to talk of feedback, adjusting designs to its possible consequences. Joseph Perrine, a visiting U.S. scholar, deserves acknowledgment for opening us to social perception, challenging the common misconception that we observe what is objectively on front of us.

Because most of these inspiring ideas were born in the United States, I knew that I would have to continue my graduate studies there. To prepare myself for that eventuality, in the summer of 1959, I interned at a design office in Oxford, England. At the famous bookstore Blackwell, I bought two books that would become important in directing my scholarly path in ways I could not imagine then. One was Ludwig Wittgenstein's (1947) *Tractatus*, the other Ross Ashby's (1956) *Introduction to Cybernetics*. I bought the first because it was written in German and English side by side—I was far from fluent in English and naively imagined it would help—and the second for growing the seeds that Rittel had planted in us.

In the fall of 1961, a Fulbright Travel Grant and a Ford International Fellowship brought me to Princeton University's Department of Psychology. I was a misfit at a prestigious university in a department that had become specialized in rat psychology almost exclusively. Hadley Cantril, a retired professor of social psychology, sympathized with my unhappiness and arranged for me to visit several leading social scientists in Boston, Cambridge, Ann Arbor, and Urbana. I talked to Jerome Bruner, George Miller, an assistant to Anatol Rapoport, and at Michigan State University, Hans Toch and David Berlo, whose academic contributions I learned to appreciate only later. The Institute for Communication Research at the University of Illinois impressed me for its interdisciplinary orientation. During my visit, I mentioned cybernetics in passing and was directed to a Biological Computer Laboratory, headed by Heinz von Foerster, whom I met in his office. When he informed me that Ashby was in Urbana and taught a two-semester course on cybernetics, this ended my search for a place to study. I became a graduate student of communication from 1962 to 1964.

I took advantage of available courses in cultural anthropology, linguistics, sociology, and social psychology. But Ashby's 1962–63 course influenced my thinking most profoundly. I was the first communication student who registered for it. My academic advisor, Howard Maclay, not only agreed to my taking a course in Electrical Engineering, where it was offered, he became so convinced of its value to communication scholarship that he encouraged several fellow students to study cybernetics as well.

UNFOLDING INVOLVEMENT

Well before the ideas of cybernetics began to energize the academic community, Ashby had worked at a British psychiatric institute on models of adaptation of the human brain. Already in the 1940s, he wrote about self-organizing systems (Ashby, 1947) followed by *Design for a Brain* (Ashby, 1952). He quickly embraced Wiener's ideas but was convinced that cybernetics would not come to fruition if it remained on Wiener's level of abstraction. *An Introduction to Cybernetics* was his response.

Therein, Ashby (1956, pp. 2–4) defined cybernetics as the study of all possible systems that are closed to organization and information but open to energy, (matter,) and perturbations from their environment. His definition of cybernetics did not follow Wiener's (1948) focus on control and communication but embraced the circularities, central to Wiener's notion of control, in his conception of systems whose organization closed them up to what they regulated. Attending to all conceivable circular forms of organization had an important epistemological dimension. It did not limit cybernetics to theorizing observations but acknowledged being informed when the systems it explored are not found in nature or cannot be built. This brought cybernetics close to being a language, not limited by what it describes. To illustrate the scope of his definition, he suggested that cybernetics relates to real systems as geometry relates to the surface of the earth. His conception opened cybernetics to enormous possibilities but also acknowledged the active role of cyberneticians in creating what they explored. As a student of social communication, this reflexivity most certainly appealed to me.

Ashby's course introduced us to several formalisms—set theory, network theory, and probability statistics—capable of tracking the dynamics of circular causal systems that could either converge to and maintain dynamic equilibria when feedback was deviation reducing or negative or escalate toward breakdowns and the emergence of unexpected structures when feedback deviation was amplifying or positive. Adaptation, information flow, intelligence amplification, and issues of complexity percolated most discussions.

Interestingly, his concept of self-organizing systems, which is echoed in his definition of cybernetics, did not get much traction until a 1960 conference dedicated to this concept (Yovits & Cameron, 1960). Foerster described this conference as a significant breakthrough in the history of cybernetics. While I was his student, Ashby searched for the meaning of "self" and concluded it to be the ability of a system to maintain its identity in the face of perturbations. From my growing social scientific perspective, I was then and am still leery with imposing a self on a system that could not articulate it (Krippendorff, 2017). However, at that time, Ashby convinced us that maintaining an identity in the face of disturbances is the behavioral manifestation of having a self.

While Ashby was a determinist when talking of machines and building mechanical prototypes for demonstrating cybernetic principles, non-determinable variety, uncertainty and noise in processes of communication of information were equally central to his teaching. He did buy into the much criticized linearity of Claude Shannon's information theory but employed his entropy measures to account for a variety of phenomena. For example, he had developed and built a model of what he called an ultra-stable system, able to qualitatively change its behavior to preserve its essential variables (i.e. its identity), when perturbed. This conception has now morphed into Artificial Intelligence (AI)'s conception of machine learning. It led him to his famous Law of Requisite Variety, which recognized that systems are viable to the extent they can mobilize internal variety equal to or larger than what perturbed them. This law generalized both Shannon's tenth theorem, fundamental to his *Mathematical Theory of Communication* (Shannon & Weaver, 1949, p. 37), and the second law of thermodynamics of physics.

Unlike other cyberneticians of his time, Ashby posed many epistemological questions. One of his explorations concerned the limits of understanding systems whose internal workings were not observable, obviously including working brains, something that most cognitive scientists fail to recognize. He pioneered the systematic study of what is now generally called "black boxes" and demonstrated that predicting their behavior to a degree better than chance is limited to systems that did not possess internal loops. As soon as systems possessed circular forms of organization, even relatively simple ones, they defied understanding from observational data. By confronting us with a machine he designed, hence knew, he made us aware of two fundamentally different approaches to understanding systems—by observing or by designing them—and he used this demonstration to justify the cybernetic method of studying complex phenomena by experimenting with models. The distinction between observability and synthesizability was later elaborated in Foerster's (1984) distinction between trivial and non-trivial machines. Most behavioral scientist at this time, B. F. Skinner for example, believed they could understand human behavior by correlating their inputs and outputs. This limited psychology to the most trivial aspects of human behavior.

Ashby's cybernetics acknowledged the triple role of cyberneticians as conceptualizers, as designers of models, and as experimenters with the models they had built, not as passive observers.

After the course, cybernetics continued to challenge several of us. We founded a cybernetics club at the university, which met once a week to digest and expand cybernetic ideas into areas in which each of us was working. Roger Conant, who was Ashby's assistant at that time, joined us as well.

I wrote my dissertation on content analysis (Krippendorff, 1967). I chose this topic because I recognized content analysis as one of two social science methodologies indigenous to communication research and somewhat underdeveloped, the other being network analysis. Ashby was on my dissertation committee. Chapters 5 and 7 of my dissertation developed qualitative information measures of the extent to which given data could inform the research question that content analysts were pursuing. The idea of research as processing information from phenomena via data to analytical results or theories carried into my later methodological contributions.

In 1964, as All But Dissertation, I started teaching graduate courses at the University of Pennsylvania's Annenberg School for (then "of") Communication. Content analysis was one of them, naturally. But the two courses I favored to teach were called "Models of Communication" and "Cybernetics and Society." The first was a conceptual introduction to communication research, following Ashby's methods of inquiry, emphasizing circular conceptions of communication and their largely ignored systemic consequences. The other concerned social systems and cybernetic conceptions of organizational phenomena. I was fortunate to be able to mentor excellent students who continued to apply cybernetic ideas in diverse social domains. James R. Taylor, John N. Clippinger, Thomas Wickenden II, Charles Goodwin, Jane Jorgenson, and Mariaelena Bartesaghi were not the only ones who pursued cybernetic paths after receiving their PhD from Annenberg. Larry Richards and Fred Steier wrote cybernetic dissertations in other departments. But I am going beyond the chronology of my involvement.

I joined the American Society for Cybernetics as soon as I had heard of its formation. Its first annual conference took place in Gaithersburg, MD. Two experiences made this 1967 conference most memorable to me: I met many cyberneticians in person whose works I knew only from the literature. Warren McCulloch signed my membership card. And I had the opportunity to listen to Margaret Mead's (1968) influential keynote address. She reminded us of the history of cybernetics, not of ancient feedback mechanisms that dominated historical accounts of cybernetics at that time, but of what actually happened at the 1946–53 Josiah Macy Jr. Foundation conferences during which cybernetics was born. She described her excitement of being part of these deliberations among cutting edge scholars. However, as an anthropologist, she began to articulate her misgivings about the increasingly narrow focus of Wiener's conception of cybernetics. It had guided the community of cyberneticians to support computational systems whose social implications had become dangerously unpredictable. Her remarks were made in the context of the ongoing Cold War with the Soviet Union (not incidentally, Russian cyberneticians participated in this conference). She was worried about the increasing automation of military defense systems by both sides and our utter inability to foresee how they would interact. She did not address issues of *Purposive Systems,* the conference theme. Instead, she observed that the language of cybernetics had spread across many spheres of life and shaped the realities we have come to live with. She called on cyberneticians to be cognizant of how they shaped their theories and suggested to equate cybernetics with the language they were using to create their realities, and, given the complexities that cybernetics had created, that this language should enable cross-disciplinary dialog. Her proposal amounted to a gestalt switch from a cybernetics of automata to a cybernetics that is practiced in dialog, to a *cybernetics of cybernetics* that could address the larger social, political, and cultural consequences of cybernetic ideas.

Mead's concerns resonated with me and Ashby's approach to cybernetics, but they got only slowly my scholarly effort to introduce cybernetics into the emerging field of communication research. Nevertheless, the first academic paper I presented to a conference of communication scholars, subsequently turned into an award-winning publication, criticized the field of communication research for dividing itself into separate domains of inquiry, unable to grasp the systemic and dynamic characteristics of communication in society (Krippendorff, 1970). It informed my subsequent efforts to move beyond the then dominant one–many conception of mass communication to circular conceptions and culminated in my proposal to conceive of cybernetics as a reflexive mode of inquiry (Krippendorff, 2008a).

It should be noted that even after acknowledging postmodernism, most social scientists still consider language as representational, as being *about* something. Social theorists tend to talk about social phenomena as if they existed independent of their describing them as such. With this epistemological stance, it is not surprising that communication theorists at that time rarely acknowledged that the subjects theorized by them do not merely provide data for social research; they are actually capable of communicating among themselves, even discussing and enacting conceptions of communication when hearing of them. In fact, publishing communication theories most likely either inspire their readers to enact them, ignore them as irrelevant to their lives, or inspire actively opposing their truth claims. For example, publishing the results of polling a population in advance of elections is well known to effect decisions to vote that can validate or invalidate the published predictions (Krippendorff, 2005). The cybernetics of theorizing social phenomena are diagrammed in Figure 1.

In Figure 1, one can identify at least three circularities common to most social inquiries. Social theories are always constructed in the language of a scholarly community, regardless of whether their theorists are unaware of how their language directs their attention to some conceptions at the expense of others. After reaching consensus on whether they answer chosen research questions, social theories are published and inform interested readers. However, those who have a stake in them will act on their interpretations, affecting the truth claims of the published theories. I would say that valid social theories have to be lived. If published and adopted by their reader, they become part of everyday circularities. For natural scientists, this may not be a problem as their objects of attention—molecules, geological formations, or galaxies—do not speak or care about how they are examined and theorized. But for social scientists, the idea that the validity of their theories could change right in front of their eyes is an epistemological nightmare. Although cyberneticians may easily

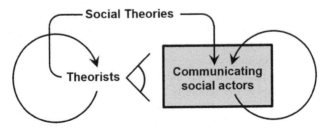

Figure 1. The three reflexive loops of self-validating or -invalidating social theories.

recognize the consequences of these circularities, Wiener's cybernetics could not address them as its mathematics had no place for the social scientists who are constitutive parts of these circularities.

Before going further into the cybernetic use of language, let me mention several concepts that encouraged this move.

Gregory Bateson (2000, pp. 405–416) was the first to recognize the evolutionary nature of Ashby's cybernetics. Recall that Ashby's cybernetics concerned the study of all conceivable self-organizing systems, which was informed or constrained only by what could not be imagined, observed, designed, or built. Inasmuch as these "negative explanations," as he called them, occur in the language of cyberneticians, Bateson linked Ashby's cybernetics to Darwin's conceptions of natural selection (elimination of the unfit) but on the level of epistemology. Accordingly, the systems of interest to cybernetics are not true or false; they were either afforded within the constraints of what is realizable or they failed. Larry Richards's dissertation took this epistemology into the domain of organization theory, suggesting to replace the narrow pursuit of organizational purposes in favor of exploring the constraints within which organizations could thrive and remain viable. Bateson framed his own opposition to the systematic pursuit of conscious purpose as destructive of the very ecology that supports being human.

Bateson caused another important shift in my thinking. While Shannon and Ashby linked information to measures of uncertainty and variety, Bateson (2000, p. 459) defined "The elementary unit of information (as) a difference which makes a difference." This mapped the conception of information into human terms and allowed him to trace the flow of meaningful differences through feedback loops, inclusive of human beings.

For Bateson, differences had to be recognized as such. For whatever reason, he was not concerned with how they came about although he always insisted that nature afforded infinite numbers of differences to be recognized. In a proposal for an epistemology for human communication (Krippendorff, 1984), I identified the missing human agency by suggesting that all differences result from acts of drawing distinctions, and the differences they bring forth call for accounts of what relates the parts distinguished. This led me to conceive of communication as an explanation of what would be lost if individuals, communities, even technical devices would be regarded as distinct entities while being part of a larger system. Acts of drawing distinctions acknowledge humans as actors (exercising options), whether as observers (creating observable differences), as speakers of a language (excluding the unnamed), as analysts (taking a whole apart) or as designers (creating components that assure the viability of a larger system). To me, the epistemology of creating accounts of differences adds to the philosophical contributions by George Spencer Brown, Francisco Varela, and Lou Kauffman, all of whom developed logical calculi for acts of drawing distinctions.

Ashby's quantitative work relates to the consequences of drawing distinctions as well. He was keenly interested in understanding complex systems and defined them in terms of the variety they possessed. To account for their complexity, he expanded Shannon's entropies into a general calculus that enabled system analysts to decompose the entropy of a large system into the sum of the entropies of its parts plus the information transmitted between them. If the parts of an apparently complex system are truly independent, one would be justified to treat the whole as a mere collection of independent parts. Otherwise, analysts of truly complex systems could aim at decompositions that minimize the complexity of the relationships between the distinguished parts, rendering their complexity manageable. Admittedly, these convenient quantifications of possible decompositions do little to help us understand human communication but their epistemology applies to social complexities as well.

I continued this work for a while, wrote computer programs to decompose large systems and presented papers, including at meetings of the Society for General Systems Research. At one of its meetings, I noticed that George Klir's systems analysis excluded all circular dependencies among the parts he identified. To me, this omission was symptomatic of the paradigmatic difference between general systems theory and cybernetics, two discourses whose contributors rarely overlapped. There are historical reasons for their divergent approaches to understanding systems. General systems theory was the brainchild of Ludwig von Bertalanffy (1968), a biologist, who proposed a hierarchical framework applicable to all systems, whether living, social, philosophical, technological, geological, or astronomical, existing on different levels of abstraction. Cybernetics, by contrast, was more concerned with circularly organized systems whose components communicated on the same level of abstraction. I took Klir's omission as a challenge to find a solution to quantify circular information flows.

Meanwhile, Ashby retired from the University of Illinois, Urbana, and proposed me as a possible successor. However, at this time, the Biological Computer Laboratory, a bastion of cybernetics at the University of Illinois, was being phased out and cybernetic developments moved elsewhere. In 1972, I presented a paper of my information theoretical results at a cybernetics meeting in Oxford, England (Krippendorff, 1974). There, Gray Walter mentioned in his keynote that Ashby had a brain tumor and was as good as dead. A Swiss attendant of this conference and former student of Ashby, Gordon Burghardt, and I were upset to hear that and decided to visit him in Birmingham. It was a short and sad visit, monitored by his wife. I gave Ashby a copy of my paper with my solution to the problem of quantifying circular information flows that Shannon had not addressed and Ashby had not solved. He thanked me and promised to read it as soon as he felt better. We probably were the last cyberneticians to see him, thank him for what he taught us, and say goodbye. Eventually, this solution became part of my (Krippendorff, 1986) book on information theory, which concluded this line of inquiry for me—except for a subsequent review of Ashby's work and my effort to quantify the computational limit and current size of cyberspace (Krippendorff, 2009a).

In 1974, with the collaboration of colleagues from six departments of the University of Pennsylvania, I organized a conference, at the Annenberg School, sponsored by the American Society for Cybernetics. It brought together over 30 contributors, largely from the social sciences, to discuss *Communication and Control in Society* (Krippendorff, 1979). At a lively dinner speech, Foerster (1979) added to Humberto Maturana's proposition "Anything said is said by an observer" his corollary one, as he called it: "Anything said is said to an observer," meant to acknowledge society. He redefined Mead's cybernetics of cybernetics as *"second-order cybernetics"* or *"The cybernetics of cybernetics or the control of control and the communication of communication"* (Foerster, 1974), incidentally without mentioning Mead. He distinguished first-order cybernetics as *the cybernetics of observed systems* from second-order cybernetics as *the cybernetics of observing systems*, and suggested that second-order cyberneticians concern themselves with their own process of observing, not with what is on front of their eyes.

Second-order cybernetics was seamlessly embraced by Foerster's equation of cognition and computation, Maturana's biological conceptions, and Ernst von Glasersfeld's radical (cognitive and hence individual) constructivism. It acknowledged the impossibility of observations without observers, insisted that observers cannot escape being part of the system they are facing, but privileged descriptive and explanatory accounts of observers' perceptions.

While I fully embraced Maturana's insistence that humans live in language and Glasersfeld showing how language influenced cognition, it took me a while to recognize that second-order cybernetics remained with one foot in enlightenment's positivist conception of science. Putting observers in the center of second-order cybernetics and celebrating the subjectivity of observations over the objectivity of what exists, did not free cybernetics from the representational use of language. Indeed, already the name "second-order" entails a commitment to levels of representation as elaborated in Bertrand Russell's theory of logical types. Moreover, Foerster's repeated assertion that "The logic of the world is the logic of the descriptions of the world" (Foerster, 1981, p. xvi) kept second-order cyberneticians stuck in being self-conscious observers, aiming at describing, explaining, or theorizing their observations. To me, second-order cybernetics abandoned Ashby's empirical epistemology of actively constructing systems within the constraints of what is realizable, Bateson's insight that the communication of differences is what matters, and Mead's call for cyberneticians to attend to the consequences of what the widespread use of cybernetics did. If their language mattered, cyberneticians had to be conceptualized as *intervening in the world with the aim of changing their observations.*

In the late 1970s, I managed to get Gregory Bateson invited to give a formal lecture at the Annenberg School. The event attracted a large audience from all over the University of Pennsylvania. He also participated in my seminar on cybernetics and society that I was teaching at that time and to which I invited all former students I could get hold of. It became a lively discussion of the virtue of family systems therapy, and of the frequent failure of individual therapists to accept the tendency of dysfunctional families to blame one of their members for all of their problems and treating him or her for a mental illness instead of identifying the pathologies in their families' communications.

Later, I became the Gregory Bateson Professor for Cybernetics, Language and Culture.

Individualizing family problems is just one example of trivializing non-trivial social phenomena. For a different example, I was invited into a working group to compare theories of human communication. I became quickly disillusioned when it became clear that the theories that its participants found worthy of discussion failed to leave spaces for the conceptions of communication of those whose communication practices were discussed. I brought my cybernetically informed epistemology into this project and wrote a paper denouncing its prevailing stance as "intellectual imperialism" and proposed "conversation" as an alternative to assuming a God's eye view (Krippendorff, 1993). Intellectual imperialism, theorizing others as inferior subjects, as unable to communicate meaningfully among themselves, God forbid with their theorists, and refusing to consider that theories of human communication should be applicable to how communication researchers communicated among themselves, seemed appalling to me, in effect supporting oppressive institutions.

In 1984, as outgoing president of the International Communication Associations, I had the opportunity to give a formal address to this growing professional association of communication scholars. I decided to take a cybernetic perspective on the ethics of constructing communication. I argued that an ethic should not be imposed by an authority (a philosopher, scientists, or religious authority) but be ethically constituted; that is, be allowed to evolve from the ground up, and in mutual respect. I proposed five imperatives,[1] inspired by Foerster's[2] two, to wean communication researchers away from the aforementioned intellectual imperialism in favor of genuine conversation. Without further comments and their wording slightly updated, they are:

Aesthetic Imperative: *Create your realities by drawing distinctions and observing the differences they make.*

Empirical Imperative: *Invent as many alternative constructions as you can and actively explore the constraints on their affordances.*

Self-Referential Imperative: *Include yourself as an active constituent of your realities.*

Ethical Imperative: *Grant others that occur in your constructions at least the same capabilities you employ in constructing them.*

Social Imperative: *When communicating with others, preserve or open new possibilities for their participation.*

MY DISCURSIVE TURN

The above developments led me to see conversation as the key to further developments of cybernetics. This section sketches my notion of conversation as a stepping stone to a cybernetics of discourse.

Conversations are commonly understood as mundane occurrences, involving a few participants interacting respectfully with one another. Conversations may occur unexpectedly, for example among people who happen to sit next to each other on a public bus or repeatedly among close acquaintances, among friends or in a family. Conversation is one of Wittgenstein's (1958) language games, probably the most important one. Conversations are performed in John Austin's (1962) sense of words being actions that make a difference.

For cyberneticians, it should not be difficult to see that conversations are *self-organizing* in the sense that they are constituted entirely by what their participants say to each other. In Wittgenstein's terms, the meanings of what is said reside in the responses elicited. There is no outside reference. Outsiders can observe people in conversations, look at videos or transcripts of them, but they cannot experience what it takes to be part of them. Conversations tend to be correlated with other activities such as eating a meal, taking a walk, making love, or working together, but they are not defined by accomplishing anything in particular.

Cyberneticians may also agree on non-trivial circularities as driving conversations. The consequences of what is said to others come back to its speaker's next turn, and multiple participants create webs of interlinked circularities. It is tempting to describe these processes in circular causal terms. However, human beings are not exactly causal machines. They do not merely exchange utterances, nor could they share their conceptions like computers share files. Uttering "I" refers to the speaker and indicates ownership of what is said. The "I" distinguishes the speaker from the "you" of an addressee. Beyond this self-other reference, as Shotter (1984) pointed out, everything said is said in anticipation of a response, in anticipation of how to respond to that response, and so on. Such *reflexive loops* account for how conversations evolve. Reflexivity is invariably present in social interactions among linguistically competent participants, but each from their own perspectives. Reflexivities are not observable, neither from inside nor outside of conversations. But they can be elicited from within by asking for accounts of them. Why-questions are prototypical requests for eliciting motivations, expectations, and explanations. Reflexivity is a non-causal circularity. It adds relational meanings to what is said. Because it cannot be explained in causal terms, nor can anyone claim to share their understanding with someone else, I deviate from the conversation theory of Gordon Pask (1975) who developed his conception from how computers interact with one another, and continued to apply computer metaphors to human involvements.

Conversations also are *the most efficient evolutionary processes* I know. Genuine conversations never repeat themselves. Nobody can predict how they evolve. All contributions are selectively expanded, collectively elaborated, and either evolve into what participants could not have developed on their own, or dropped by mutual consent. This evolutionary quality echoes Bateson's interpretation of Ashby's cybernetics, and Mead's suggestion to define cybernetics as a cross-disciplinary language able to address problems beyond the scope of its individual participants. There is much literature that suggests that virtually all technological, social, and scientific innovations are born in conversations. This resonates with my experiences as a designer and echoes the subtitle of a recent book by two cognitive scientists: "we can never think alone" (Sloman & Fernbach, 2017). They argue against the use of computer metaphors for human cognition.

Admittedly, *genuine conversations* are not easily maintained. Martin Buber, a major theorist of dialog, speaks of dialogical moments at which we can be authentic and experience the genuineness of others. However, I maintain that genuine conversation is omnipresent. It is *experienced by its absence*, in the negative, for instance, when someone talks too much, stereotypes their partners, claims superior abilities, speaks in the name of absent others, or refuses to be held accountable for what they say. Deviations from genuine conversations may well be repaired by offering clarifications or apologies.

However, when repair efforts fail or are not undertaken by consent, conversations erode into structured forms of communication: monologues as in lectures, scripted public performances, formal user instructions, and goal-directed efforts. In social organizations, networks of communications coordinate their members toward organizational objectives. Figure 2 sketches how conversations can mindlessly erode into other forms of communication. Repairing them is a mindful effort.

Discourses[3] tend to emerge when members of a community adopt specialized vocabularies and practices (Rorty, 1989) in the pursuit of particular objectives. Over time, *discourse communities* become narrowly focused to the point of being no longer able to communicate across their boundaries. Mathematicians have little to say to therapists, and lawyers cannot tell astronomers how to describe their universe, and so on. While different discourse communities may speak the same natural language, discursive practices tend to be incommensurate.

Unlike Michel Foucault (1972), who conceives of discourse as a global regimen, and unlike standard dictionary definitions of discourse as a distinct body of writing, I take discourses to be under the control of the communities that practices them within their boundary. Discourse communities organize themselves. *Self-organization* is manifest, for instance, in how communities determine the qualifications of their members, rule on the legitimacy of their

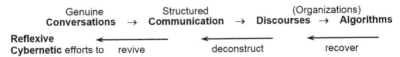

Figure 2. Erosions of conversations into communication, discourses, and algorithms.

individual contributions, and hold each other accountable for pursuing their missions. The psychiatric community licenses therapists, just as priests acquire their qualifications within religious communities. Neither certified therapists nor ordained priests have a say in how judges become qualified or medical professionals earn their doctorate.

All discourse communities construct, maintain, and advance *discursive-specific artifacts*. The community of psychotherapists constructs mental illnesses that its members can treat. Physicists propose theories they can support by experiments. Religion, philosophy, psychology, and biology offer rather different explanations of what it takes to be a human being. However, all of their artifacts—supernatural beings, philosophies, individual traits, and theories in biology—are discursive accounts that become reified by being enacted within the constraints of existing affordances. Artifacts are not found in nature. They are created in discourse. For example, autopoiesis, invented by Maturana and Francisco Varela (1973) to account for the living of biological organisms, did not exist before their "Biology of Cognition" was published and accepted within the discourse community of biologists. Ludwick Fleck (1979) traced the history of a scientific fact, of syphilis in particular, from astrological conceptions in the 15th century to modern scientific concepts. The history of scientific facts is a history of their invention, continuous revisions, and empirical validation within evolving discourse communities. Scientific facts have no discourse-independent existence and are repeatedly reexamined and revised, never final.

As for all self-organizing systems, discourse communities *define, maintain,* and *defend their own boundaries*. When artifacts happen to cross discursive boundaries, they are redefined in the recipient discourse community's terms. For example, the medieval armors, made to be worn in battle or ceremonies, become rather different artifacts when curated in a museum or under the microscope of a material scientist. For a psychoanalyst, depression is a mental disease, for a sociologist it may be evidence of oppression.

Of considerable cybernetic interest is the fact that all discourse communities *institutionalize their recurrent practices*. In scientific discourses, recurrent practices include established methods of inquiry, legitimate ways of verifying theoretical propositions, and standards for publishing findings. In the legal discourse they consist of accepted judicial procedures leading to authorized judgments of criminal offenses. Recurrent practices are taught in educational programs toward joining a discourse community. They are encoded in manuals, kept current through regular publications, and practiced in hierarchical structures of organization, divisions of labor, and may become materialized in the form of the infrastructures of a discourse community that facilitate their practices. So, religious discourses are practiced in houses of worship. Public discourses are formed in coffee houses and bars, displayed in public places, and spread through media coverage. Infrastructure can become complex. Think of the laboratories and instruments of physicists or of the organizational complexity of hospitals that are run by the community of professionals practicing medical discourse.

Recurrent practices tend to be taken for granted. Their historical origins tend to be forgotten, and the members of communities that institutionalized them hold each other accountable for reproducing them.

THE ARTIFACTS OF WIENER'S CYBERNETICS

Norbert Wiener was a mathematician and his science of *cybernetics* (Wiener, 1948) was conceived in mathematical terms. Logically tight mathematical theories easily inform technological systems. Although Wiener's futuristic popularization of cybernetics, titled *The Human Use of Human Beings* (Wiener, 1954), expressed humanist concerns, he made clear that cybernetics was not applicable to social systems. For these reasons, he had added the qualification "in the animal and machine" to his original definition of cybernetics. Neither animals nor machines speak a language like we do. Wiener recognized as much when he called speech "man's" greatest achievement and essential to social life, but then concluded that "the human interest in language seems to be an innate interest in coding and decoding, and this seems to be as nearly specifically human as any interest can be (Wiener, 1954, p. 85). Coding and decoding describe well-defined pairs of transformations involved in transmitting signals from one device to another. Language is accidental to communicating by telephone or other media, and noise in a communication channel might cause confusions but is equal to being unable to understand one another. Given his technical conception, he most likely would have dismissed Bateson's interpretation of Ashby's cybernetics, Mead's suggestions, and my cybernetics of discourse as merely metaphorical.

Mathematical conceptions of recursion, the dynamics of feedback, goal-seeking automata, networks, information transmission, and digital computation, which cyberneticians developed, generated an enormous wealth of theories, models, and applications that fueled the ongoing digital revolution. They also gave birth to numerous disciplines such as artificial intelligence (AI), computer science, robotics, cognitive science, computational linguistics, information science, complexity science, incidentally rarely crediting cybernetics as the source of their inspiration. For reasons that go beyond this article, cybernetics failed to discipline its proponents the way other discourse communities did. Consequently, the use of its theories crossed discursive boundaries freely and became the platform for the currently dominant technology. I shall conclude this article by arguing that the failure of cybernetics to own its theories is a blessing in disguise.

To understand the attractiveness of early cybernetic theories, one has to realize the close resemblance of recurrent social practices in discourse communities with the mathematics of algorithms. Recurrent practices, like work on assembly lines, repeatedly answering the same questions on the telephone, or calculating standard statistics may well originate in verbal instructions to employees, textbooks, and performance tests, but enacting them repeatedly, they tend to become mindlessly performed routines on which members of

discourse communities can rely. When recurrent practices are described in sufficient details, they resemble the step-by-step specifications of algorithms,
which when translated in computer code and installed in hardware can do the
same without human supervision.

Unlike traditional technologies that extended the dimensions of human
physical abilities— levers, hammers, guns, cranes, and airplanes, to mention
only a few—the technologies that cybernetics enabled exhibit four distinctly
different properties:

- Once implemented and set in motion, they *work essentially autono-
  mously*, on their own. Their inherent circularities render them largely
  independent from their surroundings. Even when designed to respond
  to perturbations, data, and on/off switches, they cannot represent the
  motivations of their designers or respond to the intentions of their
  users. Their autonomous operation essentially blinds them to the
  social contexts in which they operate.
- Algorithms specify *deterministic* computational steps. Notwithstanding
  the ability of computers to imitate randomness, they are unable to
  respond to unanticipated situations and cannot proceed without prede-
  fined criteria.
- Computational technologies, while built by experts, largely *escape
  their individual user's comprehension*. User interfaces do not reveal
  how they work. Even hardware and software designers have difficulties knowing what they actually do at any one moment.
- Most importantly, the very act of users relying on this technology
  amounts to *delegating their human agency to algorithms* they cannot
  fully understand.

To be clear, and drawing on the cybernetics of conversation sketched above,
human agency, like individual cognition, understanding, and intentions, is not
observable directly. Agency has to do with the ability to pursue alternative
paths, but because possibilities cannot be observed either, agency becomes evident only in accounting practices for unexpected happenings. Building on
Shotter's (1984) work on accounts, explanations and justifications do claim
agency and apologies admit it, whereas excuses deny it. Human agency is
implied in the aforementioned esthetic imperative, but becomes part of social
reality only when consensually accepted as having been decisive. For example,
for a court to find someone guilty of having committed a crime, agency must
be established first.

Let me distinguish four kinds of technologies by the kind of delegation
of agency their use entails. I call the simplest one *algorithmic aids*.
Thermostats, the apps on mobile phones, Roomba vacuum robots, data analysis software, global positioning system devices, and personal computers
expand easily tractable abilities of their individual users. The delegation of

human agency while trusting these aids is easily reversible by terminating their use.

Robotic substitutes for routine human behavior yield algorithms that call for another level of delegation. Teller machines, parking ticket automata, and online websites for making airline reservations render bank clerks, parking attendants, and travel agents, respectively, obsolete. Interfacing with robotic substitutes, while often cumbersome, may still be conceivable in terms of human play. In everyday life, it becomes increasingly difficult to bypass them, largely because of the benefits such substitutes provide to competing business and government organizations.

Voluntary or involuntary *participation in large systems* entails submitting to their technicities. Social media platforms offer users a convenient way to connect with friends but doing so feeds huge amounts of data to surveillance apparatuses aimed at influencing these participants, unknowingly. In addition, Facebook users have difficulties distinguishing whether they respond to messages generated by humans, bots, or trolls. The U.S. legal system makes extensive use of algorithms to predict recidivism (Augenstein, 2018), leaving judges in criminal cases who trust them little room but to comply with their predictions. Not just judges but also bankers, employers, government agencies, and even universities increasingly rely on computed scores of individuals that determine how they are treated. The virtual currency "Bitcoin" is just one example of a growing number of Blockchain algorithms that record the transactions of masses of people and compute the values of their subsequent transactions. People may have good reasons to participate and comply with the technicities of multi-user systems without a clue of how they are being used. Once a participant, it becomes increasingly difficult, costly, and often impossible to leave. Being prisoner in a correction facility is the extreme case of involuntary participation.

Finally, we live within *global networks of autonomous and self-organizing systems* whose installation and connections tends to have long institutional histories that few if anyone can control. We take utilities, the supply of water, food, electricity, transportation, and Internet connections for granted, not even caring to know what regulates them—until they fail and leave us few if any options. High Frequency Trading algorithms that trade stocks within seconds of noticing small market fluctuations have already ruined otherwise solvent corporations and made markets extremely volatile. In 2003, the electrical grid of the Northeastern United States collapsed in response to unexpected fluctuations. Airports had to shut down because of computer malfunction. Parts of the railroad system in Germany, hospitals in Britain, and universities in China were compromised by hackers inserting destructive code.

Evidently, the increasing networking of algorithms of growing complexity has the effect of reducing human agency to the point of total helplessness. This loss of human agency is the payment for the illusion of increasing knowledge, beneficial globalization, and stability, illusion because the systematic replacement and expansion of routine or mindless practices by incomprehensible networks of algorithms essentially ignores the social contexts of people living with them. The process of getting into this trap is reminiscent of the story of a magician's apprentice who stole the master's magical word to start a process but, unable to stop it, became its slave.

There are unquestionable benefits for accepting this entrapment. Once developed and installed, algorithms require little maintenance while continually reproducing benefits for institutions capable of keeping their users in check. Algorithms that promise to liberate us from having to pursue mindless and boring tasks turn out to merely replace them by other routines required to remain connected to incomprehensible but deemed necessary technologies that large institutions maintain. Perhaps the most importants reason for this entrapment are several commonly accepted beliefs about algorithms as being fair to everyone, processing more information faster than humans can imagine, and possessing superior intelligence.

TOWARD A REFLEXIVE CYBERNETICS

Against the background of the increasing inability to understand the sociopolitical and military consequences of implementing autonomous cybernetic technologies, and surely based on her experiences at the famous Macy Foundation conferences, Margaret Mead suggested that cyberneticians change course and consider: "Cybernetics as a cross-disciplinary language able to address the societal consequences of applying cybernetics which escape the world of increasing scientific specializations."

Except for arguing compellingly for cross-disciplinary cooperation, Mead did not really justify her proposal for cyberneticians to pay attention to their use of language, nor did she explain her misgivings with Wiener's cybernetics. It took me some time to relate her suggestion to the aforementioned entrapments that Wiener's cybernetics brought forth. Let me try to develop what I have called a reflexive cybernetics on top of Mead's suggestion and ground it in the cybernetics of discourse.

The latter suggests that all discourse communities create their discourse-specific artifacts. Without linguistic interactions, technology cannot come to be. Wiener's (1948) cybernetics inspired many. He conceived cybernetics as being *about* "control and communication in the animal and the machine" and popularized that communication is everywhere. What easily escapes everyone's attention is that talking *about* a subject matter renders the talking invisible or a mere means of focusing on something located outside language. Moreover, Wiener's cybernetics conceptualized its objects of attention in mathematical terms. His science of cybernetics made sense only when expressed in terms of the abstract/objectivist conception of language that is incapable of accounting for its social consequences when used. By contrast, a cybernetics capable of addressing what it does would have to rely on *a performative conception of language* (Wittgenstein, 1958; Austin, 1962; summarized by Cavanaugh, 2015), one that takes language as a socially constructive activity performed in public.

Mead's equation of cybernetics with a *cross-disciplinary* language implied that cybernetics could not be conceived of as a discipline like those it was to bring together. Its subject matter could no longer be "control and communication" but cross-disciplinary cooperation. It had to practice *dialog, interactions, or conversations* among stakeholders in a development. As such it had to be a reflexively driven practice. As noted above, reflexivity is a non-causal circularity in which unlike stakeholders have to acknowledge each other.

Mead was rightly worried about what cybernetics had set in motion but did not relate it to what the previous section sought to uncover, that Wiener's mathematical approach to cybernetics encouraged autonomous technologies that are essentially insensitive to the social contexts in which they are installed and create serious individual (losses of agency) and societal problems (of unpredictable vulnerabilities consequent to breakdowns). However, it should be obvious that all conversations are social and the cross-disciplinary cooperation that a reflexive cybernetics offers does *provide a social context* which Wiener's cybernetics ignored. Whether that cooperation is sufficiently generalizable to what the resulting developments come to face is an empirical question that remains to be addressed.

Regarding the practical use of reflexivity, I can report that most algorithmic aids, as defined above, are already designed in its terms. *Participatory design* in which users are invited to play a role in the developments of all kinds of artifacts, has resulted in interfaces with technological artifacts that employ icons, metaphors, and familiar gestures from their users' world. This enables them to make sufficient sense of what remains essentially incomprehensible technologies. My *Semantic Turn* (Krippendorff, 2006) is intended to wean designers away from the traditional socially insensitive functionalism. It combines insight derived from engineering, cybernetics, literature, sociology, and communication in an effort to return some of their otherwise lost agency to their users. How this approach will play out in the design of larger systems remains to be seen. In my experiences, the delicate balance between delegating and exercising human agency in the use of cybernetic artifacts is best achieved when stakeholders are cooperating in their development and use.

In other writings, I added the adjective *radical* to being *reflexive* and to being social in the pursuit of constructions (Krippendorff, 2008b), much as Glasersfeld qualified his radical constructivism. The attribute of radical is meant to indicate the commitment to bottom-up conceptions. For a reflexive cybernetics, this means grounding the historical accomplishments of cybernetics in the discursive interactions among those who made them happen. I am convinced that most contemporary cyberneticians consider it plausible to put their humanity into what they are doing. The issue is to encourage awareness of what their language constructively facilitates or systematically inhibits.

WHAT SHOULD OR CAN A REFLEXIVE CYBERNETICS DO?

Let me sketch six missions that cyberneticians are now encouraged to pursue. First and probably most important is to recognize the discursive nature of cybernetics, and *inventing new vocabularies, able to deconstruct problematic discourses and reveal their limitations or epistemological pathologies* (Bateson, 2000, pp. 486–495) which confine their practitioners' actions to narrow discursive boundaries. Disciplinary specializations have the undeniable benefit of coordinating selective competencies and pursuing missions that no one can accomplish on their own. But, as seen in Wiener's cybernetics, adopting an abstract/objectivist (non-reflexive) language to represent subject matters, and speaking, writing, and acting from a privileged God's eye position (Putnam, 1982), implicitly supports oppressive regimes, and demands submission, whether to scientific, social, or political authorities, or to celebrated technologies. The aim is to enlarge human agency.

I would not claim that a reflexive cybernetics is free of mindlessness. However, with its commitment to cross-disciplinary collaboration and without strong institutional structures that could discourage cyberneticians to question their own discourse, self-correction comes naturally. This was evident in the collective creativity during the 1946–1953 conversations in which cybernetics was born. Reflexive circularities are inherently liberating.

Second is *encouraging algorithmic literacy,* not to be confused with learning programming languages. Algorithmic literacy needs to recover the discursive origin of computational technologies and address the discursive and non-discursive social consequence of their use. Algorithmic literacy amounts to the ability to follow and eventually influence translations across discourses to where they end up to make a difference.

I am aware of several of its barriers. The discursive origins of technologies often are proprietary or hidden in their complex institutional histories. Unintended breakdowns that could reveal their workings may not occur often enough. The biggest problem is the near absence of bridges between social scientific, linguistic, and engineering scholarship in need of cooperation. However, this does not prevent encouraging examinations of how algorithms are presented publically and what they do and for whom.

Third is *promoting algorithmic transparency.* Interest in open source code is widely popular but has run into many barriers. For instance, a judge who found a model prisoner worthy of parole was confronted by an index contradicting his judgment. The judge's effort to find out how the algorithm came to its conclusion was frustrated by the proprietary nature of its algorithm (Wexler, 2017). Google's search engines and Amazon's software are so protected. However, interpreting computer programs that are publically available requires considerable algorithmic literacy, currently lacking.

Fourth is the possibility of *reverse engineering or designing alternatives* to defective systems. Reverse engineering, constructing algorithms that model the algorithms of existing technologies, is used largely to bypass copyright restrictions by competitors with the intention of improving minor features. To assemble teams able to propose human-centered and socially responsible alternatives is often costly. Nevertheless, there are discussions to find a Facebook-like platform for news that cannot be hacked.

Fifth is *challenging claims of algorithms' superior intelligence.* The idea of superior machine intelligence is the topic of science fiction and perpetuated by the discipline of AI. Notwithstanding the ability of algorithms to search through huge textual databases for documents with matching character strings, to balance an enormous number of variables according to well-defined criteria, and to mine very big data for statistical benefits of corporate actions. However, they extend mere routine and well-defined dimensions of human intelligence, like winning a chess game against a master. Equating these unquestionable accomplishments with superior intelligence leads algorithmically illiterate populations into helpless submission. Actually, AI invariably fails when situations are context sensitive and happenings are unexpected. The computer scientist Terry Winograd (Winograd & Flores, 1987) has argued for years that AI's project to replace human intelligence by machine intelligence is hopelessly misguided. He suggested that "the techniques of artificial intelligence are to the mind what bureaucracy is to human social interaction" (Winograd, 1991, p. 213). To develop appropriate vocabularies that discourage their users to surrender to the myths of that unquestionable superiority has to be part of the mission of a reflexive cybernetics.

Last is *overcoming the fallacy of ascribing agency to inanimate objects,* however complex they may be. Attributing agency to cybernetic mechanisms is a modern form of animism that grants them respect they cannot reciprocate and assumes them to possess powers they cannot exert. That fallacy is still prevalent in ordinary linguistic expressions when we say "the stone hit me." It is evident in Foucault's (1972) ascription of power to discourse, to his abstraction which can neither speak nor act. And it is built into many sociological theories, including the actor–network theory of Bruno Latour (2005) who explicitly refuses to distinguish causality and agency, explaining everything and everyone in terms of forces acting on and through them.

To be clear, substituting the job of an office worker by an algorithm cannot copy that worker's agency. Office workers can be held accountable for what they do. Programmers can be held accountable for how they translated given specifications into computer code. But algorithms cannot be held accountable for doing what they are programmed to do. They do not speak, cannot explain themselves, nor can they exercise the agency that makes humans social beings. Opposing this fallacy is liberating.

TO SUM UP

I narrated how I came to understand the importance of focusing on the language we use, ostensibly to talk about what matters to us but surreptitiously creating realities we might not be able to explain. This disconnect is amplified in the case of cybernetic artifacts whose autonomies easily escape understanding. I maintain that finding ourselves at the mercy of powerful computational technicities is nothing other than the result of having adopted a language that has no place for reflexivity in which human agency can be exercised. Judges facing an algorithm might *feel* compelled to yield to its predictions but are not *forced* to. A reflexive cybernetics should be able to identify how burdensome epistemological traps come to be and make discourse communities aware of their own involvement. This awareness comes with the adoption of new vocabularies (Rorty, 1989) and establishing their meanings in conversations among diverse stakeholders.

To me, the critical use of cybernetics is its most attractive asset. As developed above, it rests on recognizing the discursive origins of the artifacts it is able to create. To cope with their increasing complexity, it is destined to bring diverse stakeholders into creative conversations. Whenever conversations approximate genuineness, they invariably converge on a delicate balance between participants' delegating their agency to other people, practices, or machines, and exercising their agency in mutual respect.

This is what I wish to support.

NOTES

1. "An alternative paradigm" (Krippendorff, 2009b, pp. 11–36).
2. "On constructing a reality" (Foerster, 1981, pp. 288–309).
3. "Discourse as systematically constrained conversation" (Krippendorff, 2009b, pp. 217–236).

REFERENCES

Ashby, W. R. (1956). *An introduction to cybernetics*. London: Chapman & Hall.

Ashby, W. R. (1947). Principles of the self-organizing dynamic systems. *Journal of General Psychology*, 37, 125–128.

Ashby, W. R. (1952). Design for a Brain: *The origin of adaptive behavior*. London, UK: Chapman & Hall.

Augenstein, S. (2018, January). COMPAS software to predict recidivism no more accurate than crowdsourcing, study says. *Forensic Magazine*, 18. Reterived from http://smithforensic.blogspot.com/2018/01/technology-high-tech-prediction-of.html

Austin, J. L. (1962). *How to do things with words*. New York, NY: Oxford University Press.

Bateson, G. (2000). *Steps to an ecology of mind*. New York, NY: Basic Books.

Bertalanffy, L. V. (1968). *General system theory; Foundations, developments, applications*. New York, NY: George Braziller.

Cavanaugh, J. R. (2015). *Performativity*. Retrieved from http://www.oxfordbibliographies.com/view/document/obo-9780199766567/obo-9780199766567-0114.xml

Fleck, L. (1979). *Genesis and development of a scientific fact*. Chicago, IL: University of Chicago Press.

Foerster, H. V. (1974). *Cybernetics of cybernetics or the control of control and the communication of communication*. Urbana, IL: Biological Computer Laboratory, University of Illinois.

Foerster, H. V. (1979). Cybernetics of cybernetics. In K. Krippendorff (Ed.), *Communication and control in society* (pp. 3–8). New York, NY: Gordon and Breach.

Foerster, H. V. (1981). *Observing systems*. F. Varela (Ed.). Seaside, CA: Intersystem Publications.

Foerster, H. V. (1984). Principles of self-organization in a socio-managerial context. In H. Ulrich & G. J. B. Probst (Eds.). *Self-organization and management of social systems*. (pp. 2–24). Berlin, Germany: Springer.

Foucault, M. (1972). *The archeology of knowledge*. London: Travistock Publications.

Krippendorff, K. (1967). An examination of content analysis: A proposal for a framework and an information calculus for message analytic situations. PhD Dissertation. Urbana, IL: University of Illinois.

Krippendorff, K. (1970). On generating data in communication research. *Journal of Communication, 20*(3), 241–169. doi:10.1111/j.1460-2466.1970.tb00883.x

Krippendorff, K. (1974). *An algorithm for simplifying the representation of complex systems*. Conference of the International Society of Cybernetics and Systems, Oxford, England, 1972.

Krippendorff, K. (1984). An epistemological foundation for communication. *Journal of Communication, 34*(3), 21–36. doi:10.1111/j.1460-2466.1984.tb02171.x

Krippendorff, K. (1986). *Information theory: Structural models for qualitative data*. Beverly Hills, CA: Sage.

Krippendorff, K. (1993). Conversation or intellectual imperialism in comparing communication (Theories). *Communication Theory, 3*(3), 252–266. doi:10.1111/j.1468-2885.1993.tb00073.x

Krippendorff, K. (2005). The social construction of public opinion. In E. Wienand, J. Westerbarkey & A. Scholl (Eds.). *Kommunikation über Kommunikation. Theorie, Methoden und Praxis*. Festschrift für Klaus Merten. (pp. 129–149). Wiesbaden, Germany: VS-Verlag.

Krippendorff, K. (2006). *The semantic turn; A new foundation for design*. New York, NY: Taylor & Francis CRC.

Krippendorff, K. (2008a). Cybernetics's reflexive turns. *Cybernetics and Human Knowing, 15*(3–4), 173–184.

Krippendorff, K. (2008b). Towards a radically social constructivism. *Constructivist Foundation, 3*(2), 91–94.

Krippendorff, K. (2009a). Ross Ashby's information theory: A bit of history, some solutions to problems, and what we face today. *International Journal of General Systems 38*(2), 189–212. (2009) Correction of Figure 12, *International Journal of General Systems* 38(6), 667–668. doi:10.1080/03081070902993178

Krippendorff, K. (2009b). *On communicating; otherness, meaning, and information*. F. Bermeo (Ed.), New York: Routledge.

Krippendorff, K. (2017). Monologic versus dialogic distinctions of selves. *Constructivist Foundations, 13*(1), 109–112.

Krippendorff, K. (1979). *Communication and control in society*. New York: Gordon and Breach.

Latour, B. (2005). *Reassembling the social: An introduction to Actor-Network-Theory*. Oxford, UK: Oxford University Press.

Maturana, H. R., & Varela, F. J. (1973). Autopoiesis and cognition: The realization of the living. *Boston Studies in the Philosophy of Science 42*. Boston, MA: D. Reidel Publishing.

Mead, M. (1968). Cybernetics of cybernetics. In H. von Foerster (Ed.), *Purposive systems* (pp. 1–11). New York, NY: Spartan Books.

Pask, G. (1975). *Conversation, cognition and learning: A cybernetic theory and methodology*. New York, NY: Elsevier. doi:10.1080/01969727508546082

Putnam, H. (1992). *Realism with a human face.* In J. Conant (Ed.), Cambridge, MA: Harvard University Press.

Rorty, R. (1989). *Contingency, irony, and solidarity.* New York, NY: Cambridge University Press.

Shannon, C. E., & Weaver, W. (1949). *The mathematical theory of communication.* Urbana, IL: University of Illinois Press.

Shotter, J. (1984). *Social accountability and selfhood.* Oxford, UK: Basil Blackwell.

Sloman, S., & Fernbach, P. (2017). *The knowledge illusion; Why we never think alone.* New York: Riverhead Books.

Wexler, R. (2017). *Computers are harming justice. The New York Times,* Retrieved from https://www.nytimes.com/2017/06/13/opinion/how-computers-are-harming-criminal-justice.html?_r=0

Wiener, N. (1948). *Cybernetics or control and communication in the animal and machine.* Cambridge, MA: MIT Press.

Wiener, N. (1954). *The human use of human beings; Cybernetics and society.* Garden City, NY: Doubleday.

Winograd, T. (1991). Thinking machines: Can there be? Are we? In J. Sheehan & M. Sosna (Eds.), *The boundaries of humanity: Humans, animals, machines* (pp. 198–223). Berkeley, CA: University of California Press.

Winograd, T., & Flores, F. (1987). *Understanding computers and cognition: A new foundation for design.* New York, NY: Addison-Wesley.

Wittgenstein, L. (1947). *Tractatus logico-philosophicus.* London, UK: Routledge & Kegan Paul.

Wittgenstein, L. (1958). *Philosophical investigations* (3rd ed.). G. E. M. Anscombe (Tr.). New York, NY: Macmillan.

Yovits, M. C. & Cameron, S. (1960). *Self-organizing systems. Proceedings of an Interdisciplinary Conference.* New York, NY: Pergamon Press.

LIVING AND LOVING CYBERNETICS

JOCELYN CHAPMAN

How we learn to interpret our experiences influences the sorts of experiences we seek. In other words, habits of mind become habits of action. Cybernetics, as a way of thinking, changes how we act. My testimony demonstrates that the appeal of cybernetics remains strong today, for those who are lucky enough to stumble across its beauty, as I was. Cybernetics contributed to the theoretical foundation and conceptualization of my dissertation, and it positively influences my teaching, whether I am teaching cybernetics explicitly or not. While I am fortunate to be able to integrate cybernetics in my work, what delights me most is living it in my every day.

The inspiration for this collection of articles, "For the Love of Cybernetics," came from a book Alfonso Montuori (2016) edited and contributed to, *Journeys in Complexity: Autobiographical Accounts by Leading Systems and Complexity Thinkers*. After reviewing the book (Chapman, 2017), I suggested to Alfonso that he edit another collection of narratives, this time by cyberneticians. He liked the idea and suggested that I should edit the collection. I quickly agreed because I want people to know how valuable cybernetics is and to hear about it from people who know it and live it. With deep gratitude, I wish to thank all of the authors who so thoughtfully contributed to this collection.

> *Cybernetics and systems theory do not simply enrich our sense of how things work; they call for a real revision.*
>
> —Mary Catherine Bateson (2016, p. 99)

I was fortunate to discover cybernetics when I enrolled in the Transformative Studies online doctoral program at the California Institute of Integral Studies (CIIS), in 2007. The focus of Transformative Studies is on the study of how individuals, groups, and organizations change in meaningful and lasting ways. The essence of this change is a change in mind—becoming aware of conditioned beliefs, transcending limiting mindsets, and adopting more constructive, more enlightened ways of knowing. Such a change in mind necessarily transforms one's overall outlook, self-image, and direction. Cybernetics, complexity theory, and systems theory were introduced to challenge and enrich students' ways of thinking and provide a catalyst for personal transformation.

Alfonso Montuori, founder and program director of the Transformative Studies program at the time I was there, co-taught the foundation course Creative Inquiry with Bradford Keeney, a cybernetician, therapist, and spiritual healer.[1] Among their shared interests is a deep appreciation for the work of Gregory Bateson. Montuori established the Hampton Press series "Advances in Systems Theory, Complexity, and the Human Sciences," in part, to reprint Bateson's ground-breaking *Mind and Nature*, for which he wrote a foreword (Montuori, 2002). Both Montuori and Keeney published an article for "Gregory Bateson, Essays for an Ecology of Ideas," a special issue of *Cybernetics and Human Knowing*, edited by Fred Steier (Keeney, 2005a; Montuori, 2005). What was most compelling about these two outstanding teachers was their outrageous playfulness, combined with intellectual rigor. I worked hard to grasp the ideas they presented so that I could play, too.

For those who have not experienced conversation-based online education, it might be surprising to learn that online conversation is often experienced as more thoughtful and more intimate than face-to-face conversation. In these lively forums, students learned to think differently, experiencing what Gordon Pask (1972) referred to as "moments of excellence," because Pask believed that "the world of learning and knowledge does not contain enough situations that count in a valid, non-trivial, very profound sense as conversations; for there, and only there, are such moments of excellence manifest" (p. 237). Pask's premise about conversation and my experiences of "moments of excellence" in online education were the inspiration for my doctoral dissertation.

Our first reading assignment in cybernetics was *Aesthetics of Change*, by Bradford Keeney (1983). In it, Keeney carefully explains how we draw distinctions and punctuate them; the creation of cybernetic complementarities; the use of Bateson's zigzag ladder of dialectics between form and process; and other cybernetic principles, all in the context of change of mind. Keeney supports these principles with examples from family systems therapy and illuminating metalogues between an epistemologist and a therapist.

Fellow classmate Laura Ehmann and I continued studying *Aesthetics of Change* via monthly phone conversations after the rest of the class had moved on from the book. We discussed one chapter per call, while sipping whiskey and becoming dear friends. Brad Keeney told us that Warren McCullough enjoyed whiskey, too, and we joyfully interpreted this as a sign that cybernetics was a good choice for us. We joked about taking responsibility for our distinctions, for the new realities we were constructing. Playing with the principles of cybernetics was simultaneously a motivation, method, and reward for learning cybernetics.

We read and discussed many articles about cybernetics in our courses, punctuating our conversations with images, poetry, and word play. Keeney had an artful and provocative way of teaching cybernetics, which Laura and I later described this way:

> He taught it as an antidote to irresponsible, toxic thinking, as an elixir to restore wonder, and as praxis for transforming the everyday. With cybernetic principles such as feedback, recursion, and the observer in the observed, Keeney led us to experience how cybernetic thinking can take us to the heart of change to question and take responsibility for how we construct a reality and for choosing what we want to bring forth in our world. (Chapman & Ehmann, 2012)

One of the things Laura and I wanted to bring forth was a cybernetics-informed, collaboratively created dissertation. We submitted collaboratively written papers in our literature review and research methods courses, but our decision to coauthor a dissertation concerned the faculty, all of whom tried to discourage us. Somehow, we were able to win over Montuori and since he was the program director, we had a green light. Initially, Keeney was chair of our dissertation committee, but when he abruptly left CIIS Montuori graciously agreed to be chair.[2]

Our next mission was to find the required external dissertation committee member, so, with high hopes, we planned to attend the American Society for Cybernetics (ASC) 2010 conference in Troy, New York. We decided that if Lucas Pawlik was there, we would ask him first, based on our enthusiasm for his remarkable article/language game, "Forget the Observer: The Presence, the Paradox and Self-Reference" (Pawlik, 2005), and his understanding of not-knowing expressed in the article/epistemological experiment "How to Understand Giants?" (Pawlik, 2007). Unfortunately, he did not attend the conference that year. However, the ASC conference theme was "Art, Design, Mathematics—A Meta-Disciplinary Conversation" and it did indeed involve organized group discussions, which is how I was able to work with Gary Boyd, a true teacher in every sense. We got to know Paul Pangaro, too, so I asked him what he thought of Gary Boyd as a potential dissertation committee member. Paul endorsed him enthusiastically and stated that only he himself was a better choice. That was how Paul Pangaro joined our committee. Meanwhile, our enthusiasm for cybernetics only grew as we met many wonderful people at that conference: Ranulph Glanville,[3] of course, and Ray Ison, Jude Lombardi, Ben Sweeting, Candy Herr, and Tom Fischer, who wore an unforgettable jumpsuit. Lou Kauffman and Alan Stewart also come to mind. Sadly, Gary Boyd passed away several months later, on April 3, 2011.

By then Laura's husband, Ron, was progressing through the stages of dementia. Laura shared with me how cybernetics changed how she thought about and acted in his dementia. She chose to view Ron's dementia as a dynamic situation in which she could participate in a creative way, rather than as a tragic problem to solve. She stated she was often hurt by others' mindset that dementia can only be seen as a tragic problem. I witnessed how Laura was living cybernetically with Ron when the three of us spent a week together in Sedona, Arizona. Laura and I spent the mornings working on our dissertation proposal and the afternoons on outings with Ron, who liked to tell us stories about the dissertation he imagined he wrote, as well as other plausible alternate realities. When I returned to California, it occurred to me that Laura would not be able to write our dissertation now; she was going on a different adventure … with Ron. Our friendship is going strong, and she gave me tremendous support while I wrote our dissertation alone.

In order to demonstrate the influence cybernetics has had on my thinking, I offer a brief overview of my theoretical dissertation, *Teaching Into The Heart of Knowing In Online Education: Aesthetics & Pragmatics*. A more in-depth summary can be found in Kybernetes (Chapman, 2013). I built a case for my study by connecting the purpose of education to understanding processes of knowing, thus providing an organizing principle for the design and practice of online education. Although rarely designed for education, research shows that aesthetic experiences are significant in how we make sense of our lives and world (Bergmann, 1993). Aesthetic experiences are moments of acute attention, imbued with meaning, and usually felt as coherent and complete (Parrish, 2009). Their occurrence disrupts habits of thought and illuminates subjectivity, thus presenting educators with a valuable opportunity for increasing students' metacognition (i.e., awareness of one's thought process). I also seized on the important idea that nontrivial conversations are the pragmatics of knowing since knowledge is generated in conversation by how we describe our experiences of reality to ourselves and one another, seeking agreement of understanding (Fell & Russell, 1994; Pask, 1972; Scott 2001).

I then conceptualized aesthetic experience and conversation as a cybernetic complementarity—meaning a way of framing both sides of a distinction as related, without abolishing differences—and used this to discuss creative and pragmatic ways to increase possibilities for learning. Constructing cybernetic complementarities requires shifting from either/or thinking to a systemic both/and view where both sides of a distinction are unified by their relationship (Varela, 1976). I presented aesthetic experience and conversation as distinct processes that together describe the phenomenon of meaning-making. Conversation fosters and confirms comprehension. Knowing by aesthetic experience is quite different; it is our apprehension of experienced reality. It may be ambiguous, contradictory, and surprising, yet it suffuses our knowing. Gary Boyd, an educator and cybernetician, asserts the primacy of conversation to learning, but stresses that conversation is distinct yet inseparable from aesthetics and ethics. He asserts, "multi-person learning conversations are the primary ethical/moral life-world constructing ventures. Any significant human learning is not just cognitive information processing, it is moral and aesthetic co-construction of parts of our life-world" (Boyd, 2001, p. 563). Describing processes of knowing by framing aesthetic experience and conversation as a cybernetic complementarity served as a foundation for discussing ways to design online education to aid students in learning how knowledge is constructed, in learning to think differently, and to increase possibilities for "moments of excellence."

Utilizing Keeney's (1983) extension of Bateson's zigzag model for analyzing orders of epistemological analysis, I showed how aesthetic experience can be elicited, experienced, and expressed in the online learning environment. I examined online education at the action, context, and metacontext levels in these ways: aesthetic expressions that bring forth learning, aesthetic seduction that brings forth concept change and learning about learning, and aesthetic vision to bring forth or extend paradigmatic change at the educational system level. Although I mainly focused on aesthetic experience, I emphasized that the conversations in which they are interpreted are of great importance because they provide evidence of reconstructed understanding. I also make clear how all of this connects to the purpose of education as described earlier in the dissertation and how this can be designed for and practiced in the online environment.

To aid the reader in envisioning, developing, and implementing an online course or program that is rich in nontrivial conversation and aesthetic experiences, I provide a second-order feedback model.[4] I use the model to make explicit various components of interaction and their feedback channels and to show how unsuccessful interactions can be detected and where opportunities for change exist. The difficulties I address are in assessing student thinking and learning, quality of participation, teacher thinking and efficacy, and program evaluation.

I acknowledged that most online education is not conversation-based and the aesthetic realm is largely neglected, just as in traditional classrooms. However, some online teachers are finding that asynchronous text-based conversation has advantages over face-to-face education: students share more and ask more of others online, thus learning more about self and others through revelatory exchanges. Since students have only text to present and respond to, superficial differences (i.e., accent, physical features, personality, body language) that can cause withdrawal in a classroom are not present so interaction is based on ideas, with otherwise marginalized individuals participating fully (Harasim, 2000; Merryfield, 2003). I also elaborated on how online conversation is conducive to ways of teaching that invite greater creativity and spontaneity.

A significant reason to believe that online education could transform higher education is that we are seeing online teachers' thinking about education being transformed as they discover how asynchronous communication can support the development of complex thinking through conversation. My dissertation comes full circle to the researcher's role in the research—my goals and biases and the experiences that led me to this topic. I believe the online environment can foster the intimacy and spirit of exploration favorable for daring to change one's mind. I conclude with comments on how teaching into the heart of knowing is connected to love and the sacred.

After graduating from the Transformative Studies program, I was fortunate to be offered a position teaching in an online doctoral program in which cybernetics, love, and the sacred were explored whole-heartedly with equal parts rigor and imagination. Founded by Brad and Hillary Keeney, Creative Systemic Studies was a nonclinical Marriage and Family Therapy (MFT) PhD program "inspired by the cybernetic ideas and pragmatic practices that underlie the origin of systemic family therapy, using them to explore diverse contexts of change." This program, offered by the University of Louisiana at Monroe (ULM), was a magnet for students who wanted to experience and facilitate transformative change. Cybernetics served as both a theoretical foundation and catalyst for such change. For example, one course description stated:

> This course involves a deeper examination of the postmodern cybernetics of Heinz von Foerster, Francisco Varela, and others. Key topics include distinctions and complementarities, logical typing, radical constructivism, and communication, and how these relate to conceiving and conducting research that is creative, systemic and oriented toward transformative change.

In addition to theory courses, I also taught qualitative research methods and a special study elective on Gregory Bateson's (1979) *Mind and Nature.*

Creative Systemic Studies was very popular with students and I was elated to be teaching in such an exciting program. To students' dismay, when the Keeneys left the program it was converted into a traditional MFT program. I stayed on another year to help students who began the program with the Keeneys and I continue to serve on several of their dissertation committees. I also have a treasured memento of my time there. Some of my students met me at the di Rosa Art Preserve in Napa to surprise me with an award their cohort designed—a crystal trophy engraved with "Teacher of the Millennium, in recognition of your commitment to embodying the highest quality student-centered, constructivist learning: for teaching into the Heart of Knowing." In 2015, I shared the story of the rise and fall of this visionary program at an e-Learning and Innovative Pedagogies Conference in a presentation I gave with two of my students entitled, "Creative Systemic Studies: A Pioneering Online Doctoral Program for Transformative Change in the 21st Century."

The following year, 2016, I shared my enthusiasm for teaching cybernetics at the International Society for the Systems Sciences (ISSS) Conference. Former student and cybernetics-enthusiast Karen McClendon and I gave a presentation entitled "How Teaching Cybernetics, in Any Discipline, Can Bring Forth Systemic Change." We employed concepts from cybernetics—feedback, control, and distinctions—to show how the principles of cybernetics can be creatively presented and integrated into any course of study. I was delighted and honored when Ray Ison invited us to return to the 2018 ISSS Conference to lead the graduate symposium.

Currently, I am teaching in the online Transformative Leadership MA program at CIIS, where seminar-style (conversation-based) online education has flourished for a very long time. Last fall I taught a course titled "Ways of Knowing: Systems and Metaphors." For the final unit, "Act to Know: Cybernetics & Systems Thinking," I assigned Ray Ison's (2010) *Systems Practice: How To Act In A Climate Change World.* This excellent text weaves cybernetic principles throughout it; for example, "distinctions" has numerous entries in the index. In fact, when my ULM students read this book after reading a good deal of material on cybernetics, they recommended that Ison's book should be read first, as a primer on cybernetics. I was heartened by my leadership students' enthusiasm for the book; they even requested that we spend more time with it. Therefore, it is now also assigned reading in the course "The Leadership Experience: Understanding the Will to Lead" for the final unit, "Leading Change by Changing Minds, Including Our Own." I look forward to teaching with the new edition of *Systems Practice* (Ison, 2017) in the future.

I share my experiences and enthusiasm for cybernetics to show that cybernetics continues to transform individuals' thinking and behavior. Because cybernetics requires that we take responsibility for how we make meaning— for the distinctions we make, for how we interpret feedback, and for what we choose to feed back into a system—we must own our inescapable subjectivity. Cybernetics requires a paradigmatic change from objectivity to a self-referential, participatory epistemology fundamentally concerned with responsibility. The ethical significance of this may be cybernetics' greatest value. Mary Catherine Bateson (2016) stated, "What I feel about the future of cybernetics is that the ethical implications of cybernetics are so profound that we need to continue to do all that we can to influence people's thinking to be more systemic" (p. 102). By changing how we think, cybernetics transforms how we behave, thus increasing possibilities for positive systemic change.

NOTES

1. For personal narratives by Montuori and Keeney, see "Complexity and Transdisciplinarity: Reflections On Theory and Practice" (Montuori, 2013) and "Confessions of a Cybernetic Epistemologist" (Keeney, 2005b).
2. Later, Dr. Wendel Ray joined the committee. Dr. Ray is the Hanna Spyker Endowed Chair and professor of Family System Theory in the ULM Marriage and Family Therapy Program, a senior research fellow and former director of the Mental Research Institute, and founding director of the Don D. Jackson Archive of Systemic Literature.
3. Ranulph Glanville was the president of the American Society for Cybernetics (ASC) for two terms, from 2009 until his death on December 20, 2014. For a discussion on the ASC during Ranulph's tenure, see "In Ranulph's Terms" (Fischer, 2016). To learn more about Ranulph and his many contributions to cybernetics, see the festschrift papers in the special double issue of *Cybernetics & Human Knowing*, "Ranulph Glanville & How to Live the Cybernetics of Knowing" (2015), edited by S⊘ren Brier, Phillip Guddemi, and Louis H. Kauffman, also available as a book (Brier et al).
4. This is an implementation of a model template found in "Introduction to Cybernetics and the Design of Systems: Collected Models" by Dubberly and Pangaro (2010).

ORCID

Jocelyn Chapman ⓘD http://orcid.org/0000-0001-6561-8758

REFERENCES

Bateson, G. (1979). *Mind and nature: A necessary unity*. New York, NY: Dutton.

Bateson, M. C. (2016). Living in cybernetics—making it personal. *Cybernetics and Human Knowing*, 23(1), 98–101. doi:10.1108/K-11-2014-0258

Bergmann, S. (1993). An epistemological justification for aesthetic experience. *Journal of Aesthetic Education*, 27(2), 107–112. doi:10.2307/3333416

Boyd, G. (2001). Reflections on the conversation theory of Gordon Pask. *Kybernetes*, 30(5/6), 560. doi:10.1108/03684920110391788

Brier, S., Guddemi, P., & Kauffman, L. H. (2016). *Ranulph Galnville and how to live the cybernetics of unknowing* (Vol. 22, No. 2–3). Luton, UK: Andrews UK Limited.

Chapman, J. (2013). The pragmatics and aesthetics of knowing: Implications for online education. *Kybernetes*, 42(8), 1166–1180. doi:10.1108/K-06-2013-0114

Chapman, J., Ehmann, L.(2012). Becoming "we" with Brad Keeney. In R. Glanville (Ed.), *Trojan horses: A rattle bag from the "Cybernetics: Art, Design, Mathematics—A Meta-Disciplinary Conversation" post-conference workshop (echoraum ed.)*. Vienna, Austria: Wien.

Chapman, J., Ehmann, L., et al. (2012). Becoming "we" with Brad Keeney. In R. Glanville (Ed.), *Trojan horses: A rattle bag from the "Cybernetics: Art, Design, Mathematics—A Meta-Disciplinary Conversation" post-conference workshop (echoraum ed.)*. Vienna, Austria: Wien.

Dubberly, H., & Pangaro, P. (2010). *Introduction to cybernetics and the design of systems: Collected models*. Retrieved from http://pangaro.com/portfolio/pdf/Cybernetics_Book-of-Models_v4.5.pdf

Fell, L., & Russell, D. (1994). The dance of understanding. In L. Fell, D. Russell, & A. Stewart (Eds.), *Seized by agreement, swamped by understanding*. Sydney, Australia: Hawkesbury Printing.

Fischer, T. (2016). In Ranulph's terms. *Cybernetics & Human Knowing*, 23(1), 87–97.

Harasim, L. (2000). Shift happens: Online education as a new paradigm in learning. *The Internet and Higher Education*, 3(1-2), 41–61. doi:10.1016/S1096-7516(00)00032-4

Ison, R. (2017). *Systems practice: How to act: In situations of uncertainty and complexity in a climate-change world*. New York, NY: Springer.

Ison, R. (2017). Systems practice: How to act: In situations of uncertainty and complexity in a climate-change world. New York, NY: Springer.

Keeney, B. (1983). *Aesthetics of change*. New York, NY: Guildford Press.

Keeney, B. (2005b). Confessions of a cybernetic epistemologist. *Kybernetes*, 34(3/4), 373–384.

Keeney, B. (2005b). Confessions of a cybernetic epistemologist. *Kybernetes*, 34(3/4).

Merryfield, M. (2003). Like a veil: Cross-cultural experiential learning online. *Contemporary Issues in Technology and Teacher Education*, 3(2), 146–171.

Montuori, A. (2002). *Series editor's introduction Mind and Nature: A Necessary unity* (pp. xv–xviii). Cresskill, NJ: Hampton Press.

Montuori, A. (2005). Gregory Bateson and the promise of transdisciplinarity. *Cybernetics & Human Knowing*, 12(1-2), 147–158.

Montuori, A. (2016). *Journeys in complexity: Autobiographical accounts by leading systems and complexity thinkers*. London, UK: Routledge.

Parrish, P. E. (2009). Aesthetic principles for instructional design. *Educational Technology Research & Development*, 57(4), 18. doi:10.1007/s11423-007-9060-7.

Pask, G. (1972). Anti-hodmanship: A report on the state and prospects of CAI. *Programmed Learning and Educational Technology, 9*(5), 235–244. doi:10.1080/1355800720090502

Pawlik, L. (2005). Forget the observer: The presence, the paradox and self-reference. *Kybernetes, 34*(3/4), 558–566. doi:10.1108/03684920510581738

Pawlik, L. (2007). How to understand giants? *Kybernetes, 36*(7/8), 1106.

Scott, B. (2001). Gordon Pask's conversation theory: A domain independent constructivist model of human knowing. *Foundations of Science, 6*(4), 343–360.

Varela, F. (1976). Not one, not two. *The CoEvolution Quarterly (Fall), 12*, 62–67.

ON BECOMING A CYBERNETICIAN: HIGHLIGHTS AND MILESTONES

BERNARD SCOTT

In this article, I describe how I encountered cybernetics and how it became an important part of my life. I begin with an account of my time at Brunel University and also describe how I came to work with Gordon Pask, one of the few intellectuals and researchers in the UK who styled themselves as cyberneticians. To enrich my story, I include an overview of the story of cybernetics as I perceive it. Given the importance I attach to cybernetics as an intellectual tool, I end with a plea for it to be included in all educational curricula.

INTRODUCTION: ENCOUNTERING CYBERNETICS[1]

Between 1964 and 1968 I was an undergraduate at Brunel University, studying psychology. I was on a 'sandwich course', meaning that periods of study were interspersed with work placements with different kinds of organization. In my first two years of study, I accrued very mixed feelings about psychology as a scientific discipline. Only the behaviorists claimed to be fully scientific. The rest of the discipline appeared to be a ragbag of disparate topics, studied and theorized about in a wide variety of ways. The curriculum consisted of courses of lectures on largely unrelated topics: learning theory, perception, social psychology, individual differences, psychopathology, organizational psychology, and developmental psychology. The curriculum also included some lectures on sociology and social anthropology, taught as separate subjects. There was an early superficial mention of cybernetics in the lectures on learning theory but nothing substantial was covered. I was an indifferent and poorly motivated student in the midst of what I saw as a mess of a discipline, in which my teachers, espousing different paradigms, were incapable of constructive conversation with one another. It was cybernetics that eventually enabled me to make sense of this mess and inspired me to become an enthusiastic scholar.

In 1966, I had the good fortune to attend a course of lectures on cybernetics given by David Stewart, a newly appointed lecturer in the Department of Psychology. I had previously read W. Gray Walter's (1963) *The Living Brain* and Wladyslaw Sluckin's (1954) *Minds and Machines*. Both helped me appreciate the larger philosophical tradition in which problems of mind and body, freewill and determinism have been debated. I recall that Sluckin reported on developments in cybernetics and related disciplines but was not committed to cybernetics as a unifying, "transdiscipline." David Stewart's stimulating presentations helped me be aware of that possibility. I was attracted to the thesis that cybernetics is a transdiscipline. It made sense that there should be unity in diversity. It made sense that there should be a discipline as important and as general as physics but one which was complementary to it. I grasped this as the aphorism "Physics is about matter and energy; cybernetics is about control and communication." Later, I came across a similar distinction in the writings of Gregory Bateson (1972), who used the terms 'pleroma' and 'creatura' from C. G. Jung's Septem Sermones ad Mortuos (http://gnosis.org/library/7Sermons. htm, accessed 10/03/2019) which have origins in gnostic, hermetic traditions. Pleroma refers to the 'stuff' of the world as formless content. Creatura is the world of the distinctions made by observers.

I began to see how cybernetic concepts could provide explanations of psychological processes in far more sophisticated ways than those offered by the behaviorists. Thanks to David Stewart, I had the opportunity to work with the UK cybernetician, Gordon Pask. At that time, Pask was Research Director of an independent, nonprofit research organization in Richmond, Surrey: System Research Ltd. I had a 6 months' work placement there as a research assistant. Pask was the most obviously intellectually brilliant person I have ever met. I was awed just to be in his presence. I obtained a preprint of Pask's most recent paper and studied it in detail (Pask, 1966). To make sense of it, I spent many hours looking up his references and reading his earlier papers. From this reading, I gained what had eluded me thus far: an overarching, satisfying conceptual framework which allowed me to make sense of the biological, the psychological and the social in a coherent and enlightening way. I was becoming a cybernetician.

Eventually, I read W. Ross Ashby's (1956) *Introduction to Cybernetics*. I think all of us who love cybernetics have drawn inspiration from Ashby's bold declaration that "The truths of cybernetics are not conditional on their being derived from some other branch of science. Cybernetics has its own foundations" (p.1). He goes on, "Cybernetics ... ... takes as its subject-matter the domain of 'all possible machines'" (p. 2). This is followed by "Cybernetics, might, in fact, be defined as the study of systems that are open to energy but closed to information and control - systems that are 'information-tight'" (p. 4). Here Ashby is reflecting cybernetics' primary concern with circular causality and anticipating later emphases on organizational closure.

Ashby highlights two primary uses of cybernetics: "It offers a single vocabulary and a single set of concepts for representing the most diverse types of systems" and "It offers a method for the scientific treatment of the system in which complexity is outstanding and too important to be ignored" (pp. 4-5). There are perhaps those who would disagree with Ashby's claim that cybernetics provides "a single vocabulary and a single set of concepts" pointing to the enormous proliferation of specialist vocabularies and conceptual schema within the cybernetics and "systems thinking" areas. However, I suggest that in this variety, there is enormous consensus and that there is an underlying structure of primary concepts and distinctions that makes cybernetics what it is, much of which is captured in Ashby's formal approach. In 1995, I attended an international multidisciplinary conference, entitled *Einstein meets Magritte,* and witnessed much difficulty, even distress, as physicists, philosophers, artists and humanists attempted to communicate with each other about a range of issues, many of global concern. Within the larger conference there was a symposium, convened by Francis Heylighen, on *The Evolution of Complexity,* with fifty or so participants, including management scientists, biologists, systems scientists, psychologists, neuroscientists, sociologists, engineers, computer scientists and physicists. The remarkable thing about this symposium, in contrast to the main conference, was that there was much effective interdisciplinary communication. This was because all the participants did have some grounding in concepts to do with complex systems and cybernetics. Indeed, many of the participants drew directly on Ashby, himself. Thus was the master vindicated.

Further reading persuaded me not only of the value of cybernetics as a unifying transdiscipline but also that cyberneticians were not naive or trivial in their epistemologies, that there was a deep sense of metadisciplinary self-awareness in their shared enterprise. I learned that there was an informal collegiate that included, amongst others, Gregory Bateson, Warren McCulloch, Heinz von Foerster, Gordon Pask, Stafford Beer and Humberto Maturana. There appeared to be a tacit understanding that, whatever their differences, they all had a reflexive sense of responsibility for their being in the world and were united in their commitment to a common good.

The concerns with the epistemology of the observer were made explicit in a coming together of ideas in the late 1960s and early 1970s. I have alluded to some of these events in more detail elsewhere (Scott, 1996). What I have in mind are Spencer-Brown's (1969) emphasis on the primacy of the act of distinction; Gordon Pask's articulation of a cybernetic theory of conversations (Pask, 1975); Gunther's (1971) concept of life as polycontexturality: the intersection of observers' perspectives, including perspectives of others' perspectives; von Foerster's distinction between a first order cybernetics, the study of observed systems, and a second order cybernetics, the study of observing systems (von Foerster et al., 1974, p. 1); Maturana's (1970) arguments for the closure of the cognitive domain based on an account of the operational closure of the nervous system.

In 1972, Oliver Wells, editor of the cybernetics newsletter, *Artorga*[2], convened the world's first conference on self-referential systems, in London. The participants were Gotthard Gunther, Gordon Pask, Humberto Maturana,

Dionysius Kallikourdis and myself. Heinz von Foerster was unable to attend. I was fortunate to meet him, later that year, when he visited Pask's laboratory at System Research Ltd., where, following graduation, I had been invited back to work as a research assistant, and at Brunel University, where I was a post-graduate student in cybernetics.

I understood from Ashby (1956) that the abstract principles, concepts and laws of cybernetics can be applied to any category of system. From Pask, Stafford Beer, and Frank George and others, I understood the role of models and analogies in cybernetics. I saw the power to be found in formal concepts and therefore studied set theory, formal logic and the theory of computation. I acquired new distinctions and new terminology: hierarchy and heterarchy; object language and metalanguage; programing and meta-programing; process and product; serial, parallel and concurrent processes; circularity and recursion; self-organization and autopoiesis; variety and information; structure and organ-ization … and more.

As a transdiscipline, cybernetics empowered me to cross disciplinary boun-daries. This was exhilarating. I also understood other transdisciplines (systems theory, Alfred Korzybski's general semantics, synergetics) to be quite cognate with cybernetics and, at a high enough level of abstraction, homomorphic if not isomorphic with it.

I see all 'versions' of cybernetics as having a core commonality. It is a tru-ism that every scholar or practitioner will have her own narrative and ways of doing things and that these may be undergoing changes with experience and further study and reflection. What I detect with cybernetics is a commonality that evolved amongst a community of scholars, where differences in emphasis, terminology and areas of interest and practice mask underlying agreements and similarities of form.

I was inspired, eventually, to regard myself as being a cybernetician. Louis Couffignal (1960) defines cybernetics as "the art of assuring the efficacy of action." Heinz von Foerster states that "Life cannot be studied in vitro, one has to explore it in vivo." (von Foerster 2003, p. 248) and "At any moment we are free to act towards the future you desire" (von Foerster 2003, p. 206). I took these ideas to heart. There was a coming together of my professional life as a research student and my personal life, which had previously been lived in separate compartments. I became reflexively aware that I was living my theories and my lived experiences were helping my theorizing.

My 20 s and 30 s, as for many in the 1960s and 1970s, were an intense period of intellectual and personal exploration in which I was sustained, some-times tenuously, by the faith in God that I had acquired as a child and my deepening understanding and appreciation of cybernetics. I read widely, acquainting myself with Western philosophy, world history, including the his-tory of science and mathematics, and, in a somewhat haphazard way with the teachings of various faiths ('great' and esoteric) and writings about the 'occult' and shamanism.

In those years, second-order cybernetics was a touchstone that provided rational grounding. With its help, together with the insights of Ludwig Wittgenstein (1953), in particular his meta-linguistic comments about language and philosophy, I escaped from becoming enmeshed in the conceptual and terminological morass of what is frequently referred to as 'continental philosophy'. Cybernetics helped me see through the tricks and power plays of intellectual 'gamesters'. Second-order cybernetics tells us that anything said is said by or to an observer. This gives a pragmatic immediacy to what is being said and what is the intention of the communicator. I became a cybernetic shaman, a child of the living God, someone who aspires to know the true and the good. I was particularly inspired by the writings of Lao Tsu and Confucius and their followers. At heart, I remained a Christian. In 1979, while training to be a schoolteacher, I summed up much of my thinking and practice in a brief essay, "Morality and the cybernetics of moral development" (Scott, 1983).

Not everyone who studies cybernetics becomes a cybernetician who studies 'the cybernetics of cybernetics'. There are many scholars of cybernetics who look on only from their main area of practice and position themselves in the first instance as being historians, philosophers, architects, biologists, sociologists, psychologists and so on. In doing so, I believe they miss the point, the sense of what it is to be a cybernetician and a member of the cybernetics community. A recent example is Andrew Pickering, author of *The Cybernetic Brain*, whose self-imposed positioning as a philosopher and historian mars what in many ways is an admirable text. I have in mind his perfunctory, somewhat derogatory treatment of second order cybernetics in general and of Pask's conversation theory in particular. I have similar reservations about the recent biography of Warren McCulloch by Tara Abraham, *Rebel Genius*, in which the author seems to see McCulloch's enthusiasm for cybernetics as a transdiscipline to be self-aggrandizing and self-deceiving.[3] I, myself, share McCulloch's enthusiasm. The invention and creation of a new transdiscipline concerned with control and communication, cybernetics, is itself a great cybernetic achievement.

THE STORY OF CYBERNETICS

To make sense of my reminiscences, I feel I am obliged to provide some more details of my understandings of the history of cybernetics. I am not aware of any single text that gives a clear and inclusive account of the origins, early years and key later events concerning cybernetics. Here, I give a very brief summary.

The story has several possible beginnings. One common starting point is the publication, in 1943, of the paper "Behavior, purpose and teleology" by Arturo Rosenblueth, Norbert Wiener and Juliann Bigelow (Rosenblueth, Wiener, & Bigelow, 1943) and associated discussions that lead up to the Macy conferences on "feedback and circular causality in biological and social systems" convened by Warren McCulloch and held between 1946 and 1953[4]. The paper proposed that the goal-seeking behavior that could be built into mechanical systems and the goal-seeking observed in biological and psychological systems have a similar form: they are structured so that signals about achieved outcomes are "fed back" to modify inputs so that, in due course, a prescribed goal is achieved (a cup is picked up) or a desired state of affairs (the temperature of a room or of a living body) is maintained. This process is referred to as "circular causality." It was recognized at an early stage that many fields of study contain examples of these processes and that there was value in coming together in multidisciplinary fora to shed light on them, to learn from each other and to develop shared ways of talking about these phenomena. In 1948, Norbert Wiener, one of the participants, wrote a book (Wiener, 1948) that set out these ideas in a formal way that collected together many of the emerging shared conceptions and did so in a coherent way that not only facilitated interdisciplinary exchanges but also stood as a discipline in its own right: an abstract transdiscipline – the study of "control and communication in the animal and the machine." Wiener called this new discipline "cybernetics." Following the book's publication, the Macy conference participants referred to their conferences as conferences on cybernetics, keeping "feedback and circular causality in biological and social systems" as the subtitle.

As the subtitle emphasizes, there was an interest in biological and social systems. The participants were interested not only in particular mechanisms, they also looked for the general forms to be found in the dynamics and organization of complex systems (living systems, small groups and communities, cultures and societies): how they emerge and develop, how they maintain themselves as stable wholes, how they evolve and adapt in changing circumstances.

In the years following the Macy conferences, cybernetics flourished and its ideas were taken in many disciplines. Cyberneticians also found common ground with the followers of Ludwig von Bertalanffy, who were developing a general theory of systems.

By the 1970s, cybernetics, as a distinct discipline, had become marginalized. A number of reasons have been suggested for this. I believe two are particularly pertinent. The first is that, at heart, most scientists are specialists. Having taken from cybernetics what they found valuable, they concentrated on their own interests. Second, in the USA, funding for research in cybernetics became channeled towards research with more obvious relevance for military applications, notably research in artificial intelligence. Attempts to develop coherent university-based research programs in cybernetics, with attendant graduate level courses, were short-lived. However, some developments in the field that occurred in the late 1960s and early 1970s are particularly pertinent for the theme of this article.

First, it is useful to note that the early cyberneticians were sophisticated in their understanding of the role of the observer. In the terminology of Heinz von Foerster, their concerns were both first-order (with observed systems) and second-order (with observing systems). It is the observer who distinguishes a system, who selects the variables of interest and decides how to measure them. For complex, self-organizing systems this poses some particular challenges. Gordon Pask (1960) spells this out particularly clearly. Even though such a system is, by definition, state-determined, its behavior is unpredictable: it cannot be captured as trajectory in a phase space. The observer is required to update his reference frame continually and does so by becoming a participant observer. Pask cites the role of a natural historian as an exemplar of what it means to be a participant observer. A natural historian interacts with the system he observes, looking for regularities in those interactions. Pask goes as far as likening the observer's interaction with the system to that of having a conversation with the system. This insight was the seed for Pask's development of a cybernetic theory of conversations.

Second, the early cyberneticians had the reflexive awareness that in studying self-organizing systems, they were studying themselves, as individuals and as a community. Von Foerster (1960) makes this point almost as an aside. He notes: "[W]hen we […] consider ourselves to be self-organizing systems [we] may insist that introspection does not permit us to decide whether the world as we see it is 'real,' or just a phantasmagory, a dream, an illusion of our fancy" (von Foerster, 2003, p.3f). Von Foerster escapes from solipsism by asserting that an observer who distinguishes other selves must concede that, as selves, they are capable of distinguishing her. 'Reality' exists as the shared reference frame of two or more observers. In later papers[5], with elegant, succinct formalisms, von Foerster shows how, through its circular causal interactions with its environmental niche and the regularities (invariances) that it encounters, an organism comes to construct its reality as a set of 'objects' and 'events,' with itself as its own 'ultimate object.' He goes on to show how two such organisms may construe each other as fellow 'ultimate objects' and engage in communication as members of a community of observers. Von Foerster referred to this second order domain as the 'cybernetics of cybernetics.'

It should be mentioned that others had been thinking along somewhat similar lines to those of Pask and von Foerster. Maturana (1970) frames his thesis about the operational closure of the nervous system with an epistemological metacommentary about what this implies for the observer, who, as a biological system inhabiting a social milieu, has just such a nervous system. The closure of the nervous system makes clear that 'reality' for the observer is a construction consequent upon his interactions with her environmental niche (Maturana uses the term 'structural coupling' for these interactions). In other words, there is no direct access to an 'external reality.' Each observer lives in her own universe. It is by consensus and coordinated behavior that a shared world is brought forth.

In later writings (some written in collaboration with Francisco Varela), Maturana uses the term 'autopoiesis' (Greek for self-creation) to refer to what he sees as the defining feature of living systems: the moment by moment reproduction of themselves as systems that, whatever else they do (adapt, learn, evolve), must reproduce themselves as systems that reproduce themselves.

In explicating his theory of autopoiesis, Maturana makes an important distinction: the distinction between the 'structure' of a system and the 'organization' of a system. A system's structure is the configuration of its parts at a given moment in time, a snapshot picture of the system's state. The organization of a system is the set of processes that are reproduced by circular causality such that the system continues to exist as an autopoietic unity. In general, a system with this 'circular causal' property is said to be 'organizationally closed' (Maturana & Varela, 1980).

THE WORK OF MY MENTOR, GORDON PASK

Although much of what von Foerster and Maturana have to say is pertinent to humans, arguably it is Pask, the psychologist, who has given us the most comprehensive observer-based cybernetic theory of human cognition and communication. From the earliest stages of his thinking, he was aware that the human self develops and evolves in a social context and that 'consciousness' (Latin con-scio, with + know) is about both knowing with oneself and knowing with others. Throughout his writings, from the 1960s onwards there is an acknowledgement by Pask of his indebtedness to the Russian psychologist Lev Vygotsky, who argued that, as a child develops, what begins as external speech eventually becomes internalized as an inner dialog (Vygotsky, 1962).

Central in Pask's research activity was the design of 'teaching machines' and 'learning environments' that interact with a learner, in a conversational manner, and adapt to the learner's progress so as to facilitate her learning. Pask makes a distinction between a cognitive system and the 'fabric' or 'medium' that embodies it. This distinction is analogous to the distinction between programs and the computer in which they run. However, unlike the cognitivist science community, where the analogy is the basis of the thesis that both brains and computers are 'physical symbol systems', Pask is aware that this interpretation of what is a symbol is conceptually naive. He stresses how important it is to take account of the differences between brain/body systems and computing machinery. Brain/body systems are autopoietic systems, whose structure is constantly changing, whereas the structures of computers are designed to be stable. In Pask's terms, there is an interaction between a cognitive system and its embodiment. A change in the structure of the brain/body system affects cognition. Changes in thinking affect the structure of the brain/body system. It is important to note that Pask's distinction is an analytic distinction, not an ontological one. It affords a way of talking about organizationally closed 'psychosocial' systems distinct from brain/body systems and provides psychology and other social sciences with a coherent conceptual framework.[6]

DARKNESS AND LIGHTS

Pask, Maturana, Gunther, von Foerster, and other cyberneticians met regularly, often at von Foerster's Biological Computer Laboratory at the University of Illinois, at Pask's System Research Ltd. And at academic conferences. I witnessed the ways and incidents by which, over time, cybernetics was marginalized. I saw the courage and nobility with which the cyberneticians maintained their views and convictions in the face of the criticisms that they were old fashioned, misguided and defunct in the brave new world of artificial intelligence research and the emergent field of 'cognitive science.' In the sister transdiscipline, general systems theory (now referred to as 'systems science'), cybernetics was often seen as a mere specialist subdiscipline concerned with control theory. From the 1980s onwards, the 'new' sciences of complexity, systems dynamics, and artificial life arose, with a new generation of scholars largely ignorant of the intellectual roots of those sciences in cybernetics. In cognitive science (psychology, philosophy of mind, robotics), there was an increasing interest in the biology of cognition and 'enactivism,' again, with little awareness of the sources of those ideas.

The lights in this darkness have been several. Notably there has been an ongoing interest in second order cybernetics, as seen in the journals *Cybernetics and Human Knowing* and *Kybernetes*. I do not have space to do more than mention some of the key players whom I see as the second generation of cyberneticians (I became good friends with many): Stuart Umpleby, Ranulph Glanville, Paul Pangaro, Soeren Brier, Albert Mueller, Karl Mueller, Phillip Guddemi, Randall Whitaker. I should also like to draw attention to the achievements of the learned societies that have worked to keep cybernetics alive and well: the UK Cybernetics Society, the American Society for Cybernetics and Research Committee 51 (on Sociocybernetics) of the International Sociological Association.

CONCLUDING COMMENTS

As an undergraduate, encountering cybernetics transformed my approach to studying and understanding psychology. It gave psychology a conceptual coherence that, previously, I had found lacking. In later years, as my understanding of cybernetics deepened, I continued to use second order cybernetics as a foundation and framework for my work as an experimental psychologist (summarised in Scott, 1993) and my later work as a practitioner in educational psychology (Scott, 1987) and in educational technology (Scott 2001). The transdisciplinary and metadisciplinary nature of second order cybernetics empowered me to read widely in other disciplines.[7] I learned from von Foerster that "Social cybernetics must be a second-order cybernetics – a *cybernetics of cybernetics* – in order that the observer who enters the system shall be allowed to stipulate his own purpose [...] [I]f we fail to do so, we shall provide the excuses for those who want to transfer the responsibility for their own actions to somebody else" (von Foerster, 2003, p. 286).

After some fifty years of involvement with cybernetics, I am more than ever persuaded of its value for making sense of the world and as an aid for self-steering. Ashby's Law of Requisite Variety ("Only variety can destroy variety") makes clear in the simplest terms that if a system is to survive in a changing environment it must manage the variety that it faces. It must learn to identify and minimize unnecessary constraints on its actions and at the same time it must act so as to maximize (increase the variety of) its choices. For humans this applies not only to the first order variety to be found in our environmental niches but also to the second order bewildering 'wicked'[8] complexity of variety to be found in our belief systems and in our perceptions and meta-perceptions of each other. I have written about these issues elsewhere (Scott, 2012). Here I just wish to emphasize the need for what I refer to as 'education for cybernetic enlightenment.' I have outlined the curriculum for such an education in Scott (2011b).

Discussions about how best to place cybernetics within educational curricula have been going on since shortly after its inception. The (now defunct) Department of Cybernetics at Brunel University where I studied for my PhD had postgraduate students only, arguing that one needed to have a strong disciplinary base before embarking on transdisciplinary studies. I myself am a supporter of Jerome Bruner's concept of the 'spiral curriculum': "A curriculum as it develops should revisit the basic ideas repeatedly, building upon them until the student has grasped the full formal apparatus that goes with them" (Bruner, 1960, p.13); "We begin with the hypothesis that any subject can be taught effectively in some intellectually honest form to any child at any stage of development." (ibid, p.33). It makes sense to me – and I hope to the reader - that cybernetic understandings of educational processes should be used to help educate for cybernetic enlightenment. I also believe that cybernetic understandings of the human condition reveal how vital it is that those same understandings are promulgated, not just in formal educational settings but universally, as part of the 'global conversation'.

NOTES

1. In writing this article I have adapted some passages from earlier papers in which I have discussed my involvement with cybernetics. See Scott (1993, 1996, 2004, 2016). The first three are available as separate chapters in Scott (2011a).

2. There is an archive of 32 issues of *Artorga* here: https://wellcomelibrary.org/item/ b20219490#?c=0&m=0&s=0&cv=0&z=-0.1422%2C-0.0403%2C1.2843%2C0.8068 (accessed 21/07/2017). Many issues contain preprints of articles by renowned early cyberneticians. Pask was a subscriber, so I had the opportunity to read them.

3. Oddly, Abraham's account of McCulloch's life includes little of his activities as a cybernetician amongst fellow cyberneticians. There is no mention of his significant encounters with Heinz von Foerster, Stafford Beer and Gordon Pask and his achievements in obtaining funding for cybernetics related research. See McCulloch (1965).

4. The proceedings of the later Macy Coferences were published. The editors' introduction gives an interesting account of the origins and precursors of cybernetics. See Von Foerster, Mead and Teuber (1953).
5. Many of these papers are to be found in von Foerster (2003).
6. For more on this theme, see Scott (2016).
7. A propos of this, the developmental psychologist, Jean Piaget (1977, p. 136) writes, "Thus cybernetics is now the most polyvalent meeting place for physicomathematical sciences, biological sciences, and human sciences."
8. I refer here to 'wicked problems', defined as those that are difficult or impossible to solve because of incomplete, contradictory, and changing requirements that are often difficult to recognize. The use of the term 'wicked' here has come to denote resistance to resolution, rather than evil. See https://en.wikipedia.org/wiki/Wicked_problem (accessed 19/07/2017).

REFERENCES

Ashby, W. R. (1956). *An introduction to cybernetics*. London: Chapman and Hall.

Bateson, G. (1972). *Steps to an Ecology of Mind*. New York, NY: Paladin.

Bruner, J. S. (1960). *The process of education*. Harvard: Harvard University Press.

Couffignal, L. (1960). *Essai d'une definition generale de la Cybernetique, Proceedings of the Second Congress of the International Association for Cybernetics*, Paris, France: Gauthier-Villars.

Gunther, G. (1971). Life as polycontexturality. In *Collected works of the biological computer laboratory*. Peoria, IL: Illinois Blueprint Corporation.

Maturana, H. R. (1970). Neurophysiology of cognition. In Garvin, P. (Ed). *Cognition: A multiple view* (pp. 3–23). New York, NY: Spartan Books.

Maturana, H. R., & Varela, F. J. (1980). *Autopoiesis and cognition*. Dordrecht, The Netherlands: Springer.

McCulloch, W. S. (1965). *Embodiments of mind*. Cambridge, MA: MIT Press.

Pask, G. (1960). The natural history of networks. In M. C. Yovits & S. Cameron (Eds.), *Self-organizing systems* (pp. 232–261). London, UK: Pergamon Press.

Pask, G. (1966). A cybernetic model for some types of learning and mentation. In Oestreicher, H. C. & Moore, D. R., (Eds.), *Cybernetic problems in bionics* (pp. 531–585). New York: Gordon and Breach.

Pask, G. (1975). *Conversation, Cognition and Learning*. New York, NY: Elsevier.

Piaget, J. (1977). *Psychology and Epistemology*. Harmondsworth, UK: Penguin.

Rosenblueth, A., Wiener, N., & Bigelow, J. (1943). Behavior, purpose and teleology. *Philosophy of Science*, *10*(1), 18–24. doi:10.1086/286788

Scott, B. (1993). Working with Gordon: Developing and applying conversation theory (1968–1978). *Systems Research*, *10*(3), 167–182.

Scott, B. (1996). Second-order cybernetics as cognitive methodology. *Systems Research*, *13*(3), 393–406.

Scott, B. (2001). Conversation theory: A dialogic, constructivist approach to educational technology. *Cybernetics and Human Knowing*, *8*(4), 25–46.

Scott, B. (2016). Cybernetic foundations for psychology. *Constructivist Foundations*, *11*(3), 509–517.

Scott, B. (1987). Human systems, communication and educational psychology. *Educational Psychology in Practice*, *3*(2), 4–15. doi:10.1080/0266736870030203

Scott, B. (1983). Morality and the cybernetics of moral development. *International Cybernetics Newsletter*, *26*, 520–530.

Scott, B. (2004). Second order cybernetics: an historical introduction. *Kybernetes*, *33*(9/10), 1365–1378. doi:10.1108/03684920410556007

Scott, B. (2007). The cybernetics of Gordon Pask. In R. Glanville and K. H. Müller (Eds.). *Gordon pask, philosopher mechanic: An introduction to the cybernetician's cybernetician*. Vienna, Austria: WISDOM.

Scott, B. (2011a). *Explorations in Second-Order cybernetics: Reflections on cybernetics, psychology and education*. Vienna, Austria: Edition echoraum.

Scott, B. (2011b). Education for cybernetic enlightenment. *Cybernetics and Human Knowing*, *21*(1–2), 199–205.

Scott, B. (2012). Using the logic of life to reduce the complexity of life. *Cybernetics and Human Knowing*, *19*(3), 93–104.

Sluckin, W. (1954). *Minds and machines*. Harmondsworth, UK: Penguin Books.

Spencer-Brown, G. (1969). *The laws of form*. London, UK: Allen and Unwin.

Von Foerster, H. (1960). On self-organising systems and their environments. In M. C. Yovits and S. Cameron (Eds.), *Self-organising systems*. London, UK: Pergamon Press.

Von Foerster, H. (2003). *Understanding understanding: Essays on cybernetics and cognition*. Berlin, Germany: Springer-Verlag.

Von Foerster, H., Mead, M., & Teuber, H. L. (1953). *Editors' Introduction to cybernetics: Circular causal and feedback mechanisms in biological and social systems*. New York, NY: Josiah Macy, Jr Foundation.

Von Foerster, H., Abramovitz, R., Allen, R. B. et al. (eds.) (1974). *Cybernetics of cybernetics, BCL Report 73.38, Biological computer laboratory, department of electrical engineering*, Urbana, IL: University of Illinois.

Vygotsky, L. S. (1962). *Thought and language*. Cambridge MA: MIT Press.

Walter, W. G. (1963). *The Living Brain*. New York, NY: Norton & Co.

Wiener, N. (1948). *Cybernetics*. Cambridge, MA: MIT Press.

Wittgenstein, L. L. (1953). *Philosophical Investigations*. Oxford, UK: Basil Blackwell.

Index

Printed and bound by CPI Group (UK) Ltd, Croydon, CR0 4YY

01/11/2024

01782616-0013